ISBN 978-1-332-24122-4
PIBN 10303030

1 MONTH OF
FREE
READING

at

www.ForgottenBooks.com

By purchasing this book you are eligible for one month membership to ForgottenBooks.com, giving you unlimited access to our entire collection of over 700,000 titles via our web site and mobile apps.

To claim your free month visit:

www.forgottenbooks.com/free303030

English
Français
Deutsche
Italiano
Español
Português

www.forgottenbooks.com

Mythology Photography **Fiction**
Fishing Christianity **Art** Cooking
Essays Buddhism Freemasonry
Medicine **Biology** Music **Ancient
Egypt** Evolution Carpentry Physics
Dance Geology **Mathematics** Fitness
Shakespeare **Folklore** Yoga Marketing
Confidence Immortality Biographies
Poetry **Psychology** Witchcraft
Electronics Chemistry History **Law**
Accounting **Philosophy** Anthropology
Alchemy Drama Quantum Mechanics
Atheism Sexual Health **Ancient History**
Entrepreneurship Languages Sport
Paleontology Needlework Islam
Metaphysics Investment Archaeology
Parenting Statistics Criminology
Motivational

PITMAN'S COMMON COMMODITIES AND INDUSTRIES SERIES

Each book in crown 8vo, illustrated, **3/-** net

Books—From the MS. to the Bookseller. By J. L. YOUNG.

Boot and Shoe Industry, The. By J. S. HARDING, F.B.S.J.

Brushmaker, The. By WM. KIDDIER.

Carpets. By REGINALD S. BRINTON.

Cloths and the Cloth Trade. By J. A. HUNTER.

Coal: Its Origin, Method of Working, and Preparation for the Market. By FRANCIS H. WILSON, M.Inst.M.E.

Coal Tar. By A R. WARNES, F.I.C., M.I.Chem.E.

Cordage and Cordage Hemp and Fibres. By T. WOODHOUSE and P. KILGOUR.

Cotton Spinning. By A. S. WADE.

Furs and the Fur Trade. By JOHN C. SACHS.

Glass and Glass Manufacture. By P. MARSON. Revised by L. M. ANGUS-BUTTERWORTH, F.R.G.S.

Linen: From the Field to the Finished Product. By ALFRED S. MOORE.

Photography. By WILLIAM GAMBLE, F.R.P.S.

Pottery. By C. J. NOKE and H. J. PLANT.

Rubber. Production and Utilization of the Raw Product. By H. P. STEVENS, M.A., Ph.D., F.I.C., and W. H. STEVENS, A.R.C.Sc., A.I.C

Silk. Its Production and Manufacture. By LUTHER HOOPER.

Soap. Its Composition, Manufacture, and Properties. By WILLIAM H. SIMMONS, B.Sc. (Lond.), F.C.S.

Sponges. By E. J. J. CRESSWELL.

Sugar. Cane and Beet. By the late GEO. MARTINEAU, C.B., and Revised by F. C. EASTICK, M.A.

Tea. From Grower to Consumer. By A. IBBETSON.

Timber. From the Forest to Its Use in Commerce. By W. BULLOCK.

Tin and the Tin Industry. By A. H. MUNDEY.

Tobacco. From Grower to Smoker. By A. E. TANNER. Revised by E. REGINALD FAIRWEATHER

Wool. From the Raw Material to the Finished Product. By S. KERSHAW.

SIR ISAAC PITMAN & SONS, LTD. PARKER STREET, KINGSWAY W.C.2

THE TOBACCO PLANT

PITMAN'S COMMON COMMODITIES
AND INDUSTRIES

TOBACCO

FROM THE GROWER
TO THE SMOKER

BY

ARTHUR EDMUND TANNER

CHEMICAL OFFICER IN THE CUSTOMS AND EXCISE
DEPARTMENT ; AUTHOR OF " THE EXCISE TOBACCO
LAWS " ; SECRETARY TO THE INTER-DEPARTMENTAL
COMMITTEE ON " TOBACCO DRAWBACK "

FOURTH REVISED EDITION

BY

E. REGINALD FAIRWEATHER

LONDON
SIR ISAAC PITMAN & SONS, LTD.
1942

SIR ISAAC PITMAN & SONS, Ltd.

PITMAN HOUSE, PARKER STREET, KINGSWAY, LONDON, W.C.2
THE PITMAN PRESS, BATH
PITMAN HOUSE, LITTLE COLLINS STREET, MELBOURNE
UNITEERS BUILDING, RIVER VALLEY ROAD, SINGAPORE
27 BECKETTS BUILDINGS, PRESIDENT STREET, JOHANNESBURG

ASSOCIATED COMPANIES

PITMAN PUBLISHING CORPORATION
2 WEST 45TH STREET, NEW YORK
205 WEST MONROE STREET, CHICAGO

SIR ISAAC PITMAN & SONS (CANADA), Ltd.
(INCORPORATING THE COMMERCIAL TEXT BOOK COMPANY)
PITMAN HOUSE, 381–383 CHURCH STREET, TORONTO

MADE IN GREAT BRITAIN AT THE PITMAN PRESS, BATH
D2—(B.4460)

PREFACE
TO THE FOURTH EDITION

TWENTY-FOUR years after Mr. Tanner penned his story of tobacco it retains its popularity in the trade and among those who desire to know something of the history, cultivation, and manufacture of the fragrant weed. It was never intended to be a detailed picture of the tobacco industry; but it contains the boldly executed strokes of a black and white drawing pointing attention to the main essentials—an introduction to a fuller study of the subject.

This aspect of the work has been preserved, and in the preparation of the revised edition the original text has required little alteration. Naturally, the statistical matter has had to be revised considerably, but alterations in the text have been made only where necessary to bring the information up to date. Since 1912 there has been the amazing growth of the Empire tobacco industry, and in this edition will be found some reference to its development; but, as with other features which had to be included, such reference has been treated as an amplification of the story, not as an addition.

E. R. F.

January, 1937

PREFACE
TO THE FIRST EDITION

THIS little work confines itself almost entirely to the tobacco interests of the United Kingdom, the chapter on planting and curing being added to give completeness. Tobacco being a great revenue producer, possesses an interlocking of economic and fiscal interests that apply to but few articles in the United Kingdom. In this work the aim has been to make the subject so complete and reliable as to be an aid to all members of the trade, to statesmen, statisticians, students, and the public generally. All the figures given are taken from the latest Government Blue Books, viz., Customs Annual Statement of the Trade of the United Kingdom; the Customs and Excise Annual Reports; the Census of Production and the monthly reports of the Board of Trade. My long revenue experience has enabled me to write on the fiscal side with a fuller knowledge than I otherwise could have done, whilst my acquaintance with various members of the tobacco trade and their work has enabled me to make a better survey of tobacco interests than could be done were any of these advantages lacking.

I am indebted to my colleagues, Messrs. F. B. Mills and A. Richardson, for their up-to-date articles on manufacture; to my friends, Mr. James Nevin, Secretary of Messrs. R. I. Dexter & Sons, for his special cigar contribution, and Mr. P. Teofani for his cigarette chapter. My thanks are also due to those manufacturers, including Mr. D. G. Freeman, for their help in endeavouring to make this work complete and of service.

Lastly, I wish to express my obligations to my chief, Mr. J. Fleming, I.S.O., formerly chairman of the Tobacco Drawback Committee.
                                    A. E. TANNER.

BURTON-ON-TRENT,
    March. 1912

CONTENTS

CHAPTER VI

CUT TOBACCO

CHAPTER VII

ROLL, CAKE, TWIST, ETC.

CHAPTER VIII

VIRGINIAN CIGARETTES

CHAPTER IX

THE TURKISH CIGARETTE

CHAPTER X

CAVENDISH AND NEGROHEAD

CHAPTER XI

SNUFF

CHAPTER XII

THE TALE OF THE FIGURES

CHAPTER XIII
" OFFALS "   PAGE

CHAPTER XIV
SMUGGLING

CHAPTER XV
TARIFF AND LICENCE DUTIES

ILLUSTRATIONS

TOBACCO

CHAPTER I

HISTORICAL SKETCH

1560–1912

No definite date can be assigned for the introduction of tobacco into England. There can be no doubt, however, that it was during the Elizabethan era that it made its first entry on these shores. The daring sea dogs of this period, in their rapid extension of English commerce and maritime supremacy, brought home not only Spanish galleons laden with treasure, but curios of all kinds from the New World. Among them came three novelties destined to take up a permanent abode in the home life of the Englishman—the Potato, Tobacco, and the Pipe. The Spaniards had been smoking probably fifty years before Mr. Ralph Lane, Sir Walter Raleigh, and the sea dogs commenced to use tobacco. Its entry into England probably lies between 1560–65, Mr. Ralph Lane, Governor of Virginia, and Sir J. Hawkins being credited with having introduced it, but whether in the form of the seed, plant, or leaf—green or cured—is not known. In 1586, Mr. Ralph Lane brought home the " clay," and he and Raleigh originated the habit of " perfuming," " drinking," or smoking tobacco in public. The fashion soon spread. Within a very few years all England was smoking, and as the habit increased so its supposed virtues increased also. It was credited both at home and abroad with the most marvellous sanitary powers, and regarded as a panacea for every disease under the sun. In this sense Spenser,

in his *Faerie Queene,* speaks of it as " divine tobacco."
Shakespeare, however, omits all mention of the " weed."
Physicians raved about its curative powers, and " Queens
and Cardinals," says Fairholt, " bowed to their dictum,
who seemed to look upon the plant as a divine remedy
for most diseases, and so speedily propounded cures for
all that ' flesh is heir to.' "   From various applications
it was christened *Herba Panacea* and *Herba Santa.*

Queen Elizabeth had imposed an import duty of 2d.
a lb. on tobacco, but on the accession of

> " A gentleman called King James,
>   In quilted doublet and great trunk breeches,
> Who held in abhorrence tobacco and witches,"

that sapient monarch raised it to 6s. 10d. per lb., on
the ground of the physical and mental injury produced
amongst his subjects.   He alluded to the " gluttonous
exercisé " in this " evil vanitie " of those who seek to
make it even more delightful to the taste by adding
other mixtures regardless of cost.   In addition to this
impost, James issued a " Counterblaste " against
tobacco, a production full of arrogance and invective,
and covertly accusing Raleigh—*a father so generally
hated*—of having introduced it.   Its cultivation was
forbidden, as it was feared it would supplant the
growth of wheat, and so " misuse and misemploy the
soil," an idea believed in and carried out by his son
and grandson.   Even the planters of Virginia were to
be restricted to a yearly production of 100 lb.   By
exactions and prohibitions the trade was monopolized,
and in the end the "Scottish Solomon "[1] ruined the

[1] " This term," says Fairholt, " so very composedly taken
as a compliment to James was really intended for the reverse.
It was applied to him by Henry IV of France in allusion to his
mother's intimacy with David Rizzio, Solomon being the ' Son
of David.' "

TOBACCO GROWN FOR SEED PURPOSES IN SUMATRA

London Company of Virginian traders. His subjects, however, smoked more than ever.

The belief in its sanitary powers still continued, and it became ultimately mixed up with all the select remedies and quack nostrums of the age. Gradually the clergy indulged in " a quiet pipe." Charles I continued the restrictions on the import and sale of tobacco, and entertained a strong dislike to its use. The indulgence of the pipe was a profanity to the Puritan. The fumes savoured of the devil and hell. Cromwell shared in the belief that the growth of tobacco was to " misuse and misemploy the soil," and sent his troopers to trample down the crops. But smoking went on, and the Parliament of the Commonwealth in 1650 found it necessary to reimpose import duties on the produce of New England, which had been formerly admitted free. By this time tobacco had passed what may be termed its stage of persecution. Its devotees in various countries had been subjected to all kinds of insults, followed by imprisonment, barbarous cruelties, and even death. But " counterblastes," excommunications, edicts, laws, all failed in their object, whilst the more brutal resources of the tyrant with his scourge, knife, and gibbet only served the more to spread the habit and its indulgence in secret. In the end the peace-loving herb overcame the fury and hate of its persecutors, who began to realise that they had been fighting their best friend. By the time of Charles II of England, tobacco was proving a valuable ally in assisting to fill many a State coffer. It was being cultivated all over Europe and Western Asia, but Charles II prohibited its growth here in order to encourage commerce. The Act states that " it is found by experience that the tobacco planted in these parts is not so good and wholesome for the takers thereof." England mostly smoked, but both Ireland and Scotland were snuffing, the latter habit probably being copied from France, where the infamous Catherine de Medici had first set the fashion of sniffing tobacco in the form of powder as a preventive of headache. The Great Plague increased the use of tobacco, which was believed to be a preventive against that scourge. James II imposed discriminating duties in favour of Plantation tobacco, and granted a drawback allowance. Additional concessions were obtained by importers during the reign of William III. Smoking had now become general, but it was not until the reign of Anne that tobacco reached its palmiest days. The snuff-box then became the necessity of the fashionable world. Everybody smoked, chewed, or snuffed. Tobacco by this time had attained such importance, and its import trade had reached such dimensions, that it was recognized as a kind of government milch cow, and it was determined to encourage the fiscal flow. Accordingly, for the first time, a broad and liberal measure was passed, with the avowed object of encouraging and assisting the tobacco trade. In the Act there appears to be no intention of applying supervision to the home manufacture. The best snuff used at this time came principally from France and Spain, and although " purified " and doctored with various coloured earths and scented with the most exquisite perfumes, such a mixture was more or less a matter of indifference to the revenue so long as it had paid the Customs import duty. The public conscience was occasionally shocked for a few weeks when some snuff devotees were poisoned by having lead salts in their snuff, but fashion simply took an extra pinch to guard against the evil. The manufacturing of the tobacco leaves into roll, cut, and snuff at home had commenced, and the temptation was too great to resist " ekeing out the hogshead." Accordingly, the leaves of the forest were requisitioned for this purpose. In a short time from the passing of the 12 Anne, cap. 8, the adulteration of the " arranoco and sweet scented tobaccos " had assumed considerable magnitude, so much so that its influence began to tell upon the revenue. The fiscal flow from tobacco was not in proportion to the quantity consumed, and, on inquiry, it was found that a regular trade had sprung up of cutting, curing, manufacturing and supplying various leaves and herbs to resemble the genuine article. In the case of snuff, the sophisticator had not only taken a leaf from the Spanish book and added his own ochre, " umbre," " fustick," and yellow ebony, but had further increased the titillating effect by appropriately adding " touchwood." The loss of revenue which these practices involved, determined the government to fight the evil, and in the first year of the reign of George I, an Act was passed to " prevent the mischiefs by manufacturing leaves or other things to resemble tobacco, and the abuses in making and mixing of snuff." In this pure tobacco Act of George I, or rather of Walpole, the snuff manufacturers were allowed to use water tinged with Venetian red, such artificial colouring being considered a necessity at this time and for many years after. No control or supervision of the manufacture was laid down, but proceedings were to be taken on a special warrant granted by two Justices of the Peace. Some of the snuff manufacturers attempted to construe the Act as applying only to tobacco, but a further promulgation from Walpole made it clear that it was the intention of the government to include the snuff sophisticator. On the collapse of the South Sea Bubble, Walpole became First Lord of the Treasury, and the following year saw the amalgamation of the Scottish and English Boards of Customs, and further concessions granted to the trade. The duty was now 6⅓d. per lb. More provisions regulating the tobacco trade were issued, and in 1733 the great finance minister introduced his Excise Bill, with the object of checking smuggling and facilitating the tobacco import trade. The measure was ultimately withdrawn on account of an "opposition more factious and nnprincipled than has ever disgraced English politics." To vindicate the action taken by Walpole, a special committee was appointed the following year, to inquire into the "Frauds and Abuses in the Customs" in connection with the tobacco trade, and some very ugly disclosures of collusion, bribery, and wholesale fraud were made. The loss to the revenue amounted to about one-third of the duty. Walpole may be said to be the great tobacco minister, for not only did he endeavour to suppress abuses, but he encouraged, facilitated, and developed the tobacco industry. He laid down principles which, had they been carried out at the time, would have "made London a free port and doubled English trade." With a widespread system of smuggling to contend against, even with tobacco at a duty of 6⅓d. per lb., the question of the fiscal loss involved through the addition of adulterants to tobacco sank into insignificance. To smuggle tobacco was a far easier and safer plan than to adulterate it. It was a long time, however, after the experience of Walpole, before ministers could be induced to legislate on this inflammatory subject. Meanwhile, abuses grew and flourished. Emboldened by the success of the smuggler, the adulterator began to rob the revenue by obtaining drawback on all kinds of rubbish incorporated with the tobacco exported. The increase of smuggling, however, was fast ruining the legitimate trade, and the fiscal loss involved ultimately induced the Pelham Ministry, in

1751, to pass a measure for the " more effectual securing the tobacco duties." In it a clause was inserted aiming at the illicit practices at home. " Anything whatever," found in tobacco on being exported was made forfeitable, and a £50 fine imposed for every package adulterated. This clause exercised a practical check on the exportation of walnut and other leaves with tobacco, but inasmuch as there was no supervision of any kind in the home manufacture, the practice of cutting, curing, and blending such leaves with tobacco was left entirely to the dishonesty of the trader. The greater evil of the tobacco trade remained unchecked, and ministry after ministry did its utmost to cope with the lawlessness of the smuggler. The Parliamentary Committee of 1783–4, appointed by William Pitt to report on the illicit practices used in defrauding the revenue, disclosed a gigantic system of smuggling and fraud. A period of complete demoralization had set in, and public credit stood at its lowest ebb. Everybody, from the pedlar to the merchant, seemed possessed with the common desire of defrauding the revenue. Relanding of goods, fraudulent drawbacks, collusions between underpaid officers and illicit traders, bands of armed ruffians escorting smuggled goods inland and openly defying the revenue officers, every coast town a nest of robbers, were notorious facts ; whilst inland, distillers and such other traders as the makers of starch, soap, candles, etc., were vying with each other in their efforts at illicit gain. The quantity of tobacco smuggled is not computed; probably the modesty of the committee stood in the way of stating the amount. The duty was 1s. 3d. per lb., its value apart from duty 3d. per lb. As the inducement was in the proportion of five to one, success in smuggling two hogsheads amply compensated for the loss of the other three

The American War of Independence caused a dearth of Virginian tobacco, and manufacturers bought their leaf where they could get it. About this time Scotland began to grow it. The Act of Charles II simply prohibited its culture in England and Ireland. The imposition of a duty, however, soon extinguished the Scot's profits. The scarcity of leaf tobacco, coupled with the great demand for the article, presented too tempting an occasion for the manufacturer' to resist adding other smokable leaves. It was a case of " needs must where the elderly gentleman drives." The gathering, cutting, and curing of leaves from the English woods and gardens became a system, and to facilitate the deception the shag was dyed and stained. To impart an agreeable odour and colour to the snuff used at this time, various woods were imported from South America, and ground up and mixed with earth, clay, " oaker, umber and fustick." Even the finest snuffs were impure. As Act after Act failed to secure the revenue, William Pitt determined on more drastic measures. In the case of tobacco, the committee of 1783 recommended Walpole's discarded scheme. Pitt adopted it. The warehouse system, despised by the opponents of Walpole, was instituted, and, in addition, the manufacturing operations and stock of every tobacco dealer were placed under the control of the Excise. Even the retailer came under the official eye, and it was not until the tobacco was placed in the consumer's pouch that the Excise officers ceased to trouble about it. Pitt crushed the armed vessels and bands of smugglers by force. All tobacco found in transit, unaccompanied by permit, was forfeited. Within a year considerably over a million extra pounds of tobacco paid duty. In two years not only was the public credit restored, but there was a surplus of a million sterling in the Treasury. If

Pitt's hand was heavy on the smuggler it was meant to be equally so on the adulterator. The minister insisted on the supply of real tobacco and nothing else, and from that day to this the Excise officer may be said to have championed the cause of the purity of the poor man's shag and roll. Another Select Committee of the House of Commons was appointed in 1816 to inquire into the policy of permitting the home culture of tobacco. It recommended, on fiscal grounds, the continuance of the laws prohibiting its growth here. In 1821 it was deemed necessary to emphasize that part of Pitt's Act dealing with adulteration. The law permitted the practice of tinging the tobacco and snuff with colouring and flavouring matter, and some manufacturers had " tinged " in a very liberal manner indeed. Henceforth the quantity of these added bodies was limited. The year 1830 saw another Select Committee of the House of Commons on the growth question, with Sir Henry Parnell, Bart., as chairman. By this time it began to be realized that although Pitt's Act had suppressed the more glaring abuses, the Excise system of survey, etc., had not achieved its purpose of suppressing the evils of adulteration and smuggling. Water, slightly coloured, had been allowed to be added to tobacco and snuff. Under cover of this permission, some manufacturers were adding molasses, treacle, and sugar. The occasion was convenient for convincing the trade that the Board of Excise was determined to enforce the law, and in the spring of 1835 a General Order was issued which interdicted the use of these unlawful ingredients. In consequence, discontent at the continuance of the existing regulations began to gather force, and clamours for their abolition were heard from all sides. The trade felt strongly, after the Parnell report, that the vexatious and restrictive laws had oppressed them long enough.

The grievances of the trade were brought before Parliament, but the ministry under Lord Melbourne hesitated to interfere with tobacco, as it was an increasing source of revenue. The cost of the expedition to Afghanistan, and the war with China in 1839, forced the Government in the following year to impose an extra 5 per cent on all licence duties, and all hopes of a reduction of the tobacco duty died away. Determined to get something, the attention of the trade was directed to the abolition of the Adulteration Clauses of the Excise laws, and strong complaints arose of underselling due to the introduction of illegal ingredients. The honest trader was alleged to be at the mercy of the adulterator, and petitions flowed in to the House of Commons. The manufacturers at last induced Mr. Baring, the Chancellor of the Exchequer, to stir in the matter.

In the summer of 1840, the Excise survey on tobacco was discontinued by the 3 and 4 Vic., cap. 18, known as The Mixing Act. It permitted anything to be added to tobacco except the leaves of trees, plants, and herbs. The enactment may be said to have been the adulterator's triumph. The manufacturers, left to themselves, began to use various ingredients, but principally saccharine matter. Prices were reduced, and as competition set in, more sweetening was added, until in some cases the shag and roll sold were more in the nature of confectionery than tobacco. The proportion of sugar, honey, molasses, treacle, liquorice, salt, nitre, etc., used, ranged from 50 to 60 per cent. Even the dealers could not refrain from improving on the manufacturers' finished product.

Truly, the Mixing Act may be said to have educated the tobacco trade in adulteration. No complaints were heard at this period, the manufacturers and dealers being satisfied with the new order of things. In the autumn of 1841, Sir Robert Peel came into office, and Mr. Goulburn, the new Chancellor of the Exchequer, began to view with alarm the falling receipts from tobacco. The falling off might, however, have been due to the depressed condition at that time of the working classes, but further consideration increased the Chancellor's distrust. He was paying the adulterator a drawback of 3s. a lb. on his confectionary tobacco. This robbery of the revenue at both ends, decided the Chancellor to stop the " evil practice." The average import in the two adulterating years was 1,442,140 lb. less than the average of the two preceding years, or a deficiency equal to 6 per cent. On the 10th of August, 1842, The Pure Tobacco Act (5 and 6 Vict., cap. 93) was passed, strongly opposed by members of the tobacco trade. This law is now in force. It restricted the manufacturer to the use of tobacco and water only. In the manufacture of snuff it permitted the use of alkaline salts, with lime water in addition to Welsh and Irish snuffs. It further allowed the scenting of snuff, and the use of oil in making up roll tobacco. Any tobacco and snuff " which on examination shall be found to contain any other material, liquid, substance, matter, or thing, shall be forfeited," and £200 besides. Likewise any sugar, honey, leaves, etc., found on entered premises, and any imitations of tobacco or snuff were forfeitable. Officers were empowered to sample " at any time they shall see fit." The Act brought a sweeping reform, and the manufacturers strongly complained to the Chancellor of the Exchequer of its revolutionary clauses. They alleged that from time immemorial many articles were allowed to be used to give colour and flavour to tobacco and snuff, without the least imputation of their having been used as adulterants. Moreover, " adulterated goods cannot be detected." "Our hope," said a manufacturer, "in the efficiency of the present law, is dependent upon the power of analysis to detect adulteration. Without that, we feel that the present law is as inefficient as any preceding one."

The passing of The Pure Tobacco Act brought the Commissioners of Excise face to face with the need for scientific aid. The necessity of the hour brought the man. To the great honour of the department, George Phillips, an Excise officer, came forth with his microscope and crucible, and commenced to trace out the adulterator. In this way the Inland Revenue Laboratory, now called the Government Laboratory, was originated. Most members of the tobacco trade were strongly of opinion that adulteration up to 5 per cent could not be detected by analysis, and they laughed at the idea of the Excise chemist detecting sugar in tobacco. The laughter of some, however, quickly died away. Visits of inspection were made to the manufactories throughout the United Kingdom. Before the year expired considerable seizures took place, convictions were obtained, and 30,000 lb. of adulterated tobacco were seized in the counties of Lancashire and Yorkshire alone. A glance at the ingredients used at this period reveals sugar, ranging from 1 to 25 per cent, rhubarb, hop, and oak leaves, but no cabbage. Earths and mineral matter of various kinds were used, and in one factory no less than a ton of sand was seized. Many retailers were convicted for selling the sophisticated article, a result which greatly pleased the law-abiding portion of the trade. Unfortunately, the vigilance and distribution of the Coastguard at this time were not altogether effective, and although large seizures were made, considerable quantities of smuggled leaf tobacco found their way into manufacturers' stocks. Prices gradually fell, and loud and general complaints were made by the trade of the prevalence of smuggling and adulteration. It was repeatedly alleged that nothing but a considerable reduction of the duty would remedy matters. Once more agitation became rife, and petitions flowed in to the House of Commons. Finally, on the 11th of March, 1844, a Select Committee was appointed to examine into the present state of the tobacco trade, with a view to remedy the evils complained of, and, without impairing the revenue, to promote the general interests of the trade. Mr. Joseph Hume was appointed chairman. The Committee sat for over five months, and received evidence from all classes directly and indirectly connected with the tobacco trade. Even smugglers were examined. Heads of the Excise, Customs, and Coastguard Departments attended and gave evidence, and the aid of scientists of known reputation was also requisitioned. In the end, seeing the impracticability of advising the House of Commons upon the subject referred to them, the Committee dissolved. This lame and inconclusive result was a bitter disappointment to the members of the tobacco trade, who were led to believe that something practical would result from the labours of the Committee.

From time to time leading manufacturers pressed forward their claims before M.P.'s at every conceivable opportunity ; but by 1848 even the heads of the Financial Reform Movement (Mr. Cobden, etc.) gave up all idea of interfering with this large and important source of revenue. The distrust in the ability of the Board of Excise to protect the trade from sophistication continued, and led to the formation of a society in 1851, by the tobacco manufacturers of Glasgow, having for its object the detection and exposure of attempts to adulterate tobacco and snuff.

A matter of some interest to the tobacco trade occurred in the summer of 1856 in the transfer of the Coastguard service from the control of the Customs to that of the Admiralty department, a movement that resulted in increased efficiency in coping with the smuggler.

With the question of adulteration brought so prominently before the public in the decade 1850–60, it was naturally to be expected that additional efforts would be made by the Board of Inland Revenue to detect and suppress the sophistication of articles, over the manufacture of which they exercised super-vision. Snuff especially came in for increased atten-tion. In the case of tobacco they were able to report that "adulteration is now seldom attempted." The list of discovered ingredients, however, at this time was long enough to warrant the belief that when the tobacco manufacturers did attempt to adulterate, it was no "half measures" with them. One striking instance˙ was a case of "roll" consisting chiefly of cabbage leaves, the outside covering only being tobacco. The American War of Secession in 1861, by its inter-ference with the supply of Virginian tobacco, compelled the manufacturers to obtain substitutes from Japan, China, and other parts, and scents were resorted to for the purpose of disguising the flavour of the inferior qualities. The Virginia tobacco has never since ousted its rivals, and the "substitutes" are still with us. The year 1863 was a memorable one to the tobacco trade. Mr. Gladstone, then Chancellor of the Exchequer in the Ministry of Lord Palmerston, introduced a great and comprehensive measure of reform in the tobacco duties and laws. He introduced a Bill under which the home manufacturers could make sweetened tobacco, known as "Cavendish and Negrohead," in bond, a privilege hitherto denied them. He proposed the adjustment of

the import duties on manufactured articles, notably
cigars, and laid down a scientific basis establishing the
amount of drawback payable on the export of tobacco
and snuff.   The Bill became the Manufactured Tobacco
Act of 1863.   The effect of its various provisions will
be discussed in this work under such articles as
" The Cigar," " Offal Snuff," " Cavendish and Negrohead."

In 1867 the 30 and 31 Vict., cap. 90, was passed, which
restricted the use of lime-water to within very narrow
limits (see article on " Snuff").   From this period
onwards, it is characteristic that the form in which adulteration was carried on was by taking advantage of
concessions allowed in Tobacco Acts.   The abuse of the
permission to use lime-water is a case in point.   Later
on it was alkaline salts, to be succeeded by oil and,
subsequently, water.   In each case the official curb had
to be applied in order to keep those implicated within
proper bounds.   With regard to alkaline salts, the 5 and
6 Vict., cap. 93, s. 1, permitted their use in snuff, but
did not define them nor fix a limit as to the quantity to
be used.   Directly the use of lime-water was restricted,
a rush to these alkaline substances was made.   In the
following year quantities of carbonate of soda, ranging
from 33 to 57 per cent. in weight, were found in some
snuffs, " a most flagrant and reprehensible abuse of the
law."   The whitish appearance imparted to snuff by
this excessive " salting " was neutralized by the addition
of colouring matter, such as the red oxide of iron.   The
manufacturers in Ireland still gave a great deal of
trouble.

In 1871 a deputation of manufacturers emphasized the
public reliance placed on the chemical staff, and the
presence of the former that day in the Board Room
asking for protection, and undertaking in future to

co-operate with the Excise officers, may be said to have been a great moral victory for the Board.

Some of the smaller manufacturers could not be induced to give up wholly the use of gum arabic. Unable to compete with the larger manufacturers in their improved methods, attempts were made to imitate the superior kinds of " Irish roll," which now had become popular, by adding gum and also colouring matter.

The year 1878 brought some unpleasant surprises to the tobacco trade. The Government of Lord Beaconsfield wanted money, in order to provide funds for the " vote of credit " during the war between Russia and Turkey. Accordingly, the import duties on tobacco were increased by 4d. per pound (farthing per ounce). On an attempt being made by some retailers to charge the working-man $3\frac{1}{4}$d. for his ounce of shag, the latter refused to pay more than the time-honoured 3d., whilst in other cases the farthing was found to be too inconvenient a coin to trade with. The members of the retail trade thereupon insisted on the manufacturer supplying them with goods at the old prices, and as the latter was also compelled to pay the additional fourpence, he was placed betwixt the hammer and the anvil. Fortunately, at this time the price of leaf was low, and he was better able to meet the demand. To meet future contingencies he purchased inferior leaf, and adopted the stratagem of some publicans and dairymen of resorting to the pump. Thus, by selling an inferior and a wetter article, he was enabled to meet the dual demands made by the Government and the retailer, and to partly recoup himself at the same time. Another cause of serious apprehension to the trade this year was the legislative clause 41 Vict., cap. 15, s. 25, which restricted the use of alkaline salts in the manufacture of snuff, and enumerated those allowed in future to be added. (See article on " Snuff.")

From the question of salts in snuff, the attention of the Board of Inland Revenue was next directed to that of oil in roll. Under the Pure Tobacco Act of 1842 (5 and 6 Vict., cap. 93) permission was given to use oil in making up spun or roll tobacco. Nothing but water and oil was allowed to be present in this class of tobacco. The oil not being specified, various kinds were ultimately used, some with the object of increasing the weight, and others the flavour of the roll and the similar article—cake cavendish. As a safeguard to the revenue, the Board deemed it necessary to name the kind allowed to be used. The opportunity was given the trade to state the particular oil preferred, and " olive oil " was selected, on account of its being non-drying, " fixed," or non-volatile, and not liable to " crack," or decompose at the high temperature of the baking-stove. The new clause of the Customs and Inland Revenue Act of 1879 therefore disallowed all oil " other than essential oil for the purpose of flavouring, and olive oil in the process of spinning and rolling up the tobacco."

The practice of adding excessive quantities of water to tobacco increased. No limit to the quantity that might be present in the shag or roll was laid down, and a great demand sprang up for dry " spongy " classes of inferior leaf, capable of absorbing large quantities of moisture. Such varieties as " Java," which absorb from 40 to 50 per cent of water, were in special request. The production of such a wet article considerably reduced the clearances of leaf from the Customs warehouses, and although deputation after deputation from the trade drew the attention of the Government to this and other evils ensuing from the increased impost, the " obnoxious " 4d. remained. Even in 1881 sufficient time had not been deemed to have elapsed for the Government to pronounce whether the fiscal experiment was a failure or not. The manufacturers continued to agitate for the repeal of this 4d., and now and then rumours of a statutory restriction of moisture circulated amongst them, the fear of such probably being father to the thought. If the various meetings and discussions were futile in achieving the purpose in view, they yet revealed to the members of the trade their strength. The need of combination and co-operation was forced home by this last vexatious increase of duty, and in the spring of 1884 an organising of members took place, and, in addition, a Tobacco Section was formed in connection with the London Chamber of Commerce, for the purpose of protecting the trade.

In 1886, with a view to assist the agricultural interest, the Government permitted approved persons to make experiments as to whether tobacco could be successfully cultivated in the United Kingdom. The experiments were conducted under special conditions, and were continued for several years, being distributed over twenty-seven counties. About twenty-three acres were planted in 1887, the number of cultivators being fifty-seven. The tobacco produced was rank in flavour and of poor quality, being inferior to the commonest varieties of leaf imported into this country. As duty was charged at the same rate as that on imported tobacco, the cultivation was found to be unprofitable and was for many years abandoned.

In 1887, on Budget night, Mr. Goschen, the Chancellor of the Exchequer, announced the repeal of the " obnoxious 4d.," and candidly admitted that its imposition nine years before was an error. The proposed change was warmly welcomed by members of the tobacco trade, who from the first had felt the increased duty to be a mischievous piece of legislation. Besides failing in its object, it had harassed the trade, and

resulted in the production of a debased article, with
an actual decrease in the consumption per head.   In
the reduction of the duty by the small sum of 4d., the
difficulty lay in ensuring that the working man should
have the benefit of the decrease by getting a better
article for his money.   How this was to be done is best
told in Mr. Goschen's own words—" The natural
moisture of tobacco is from 15 to 17 per cent, and it is
increased to 30 per cent in process of manufacture.
But now it is often sold containing 40 or 45 per cent
of water.   In future, we intend to make it illegal to sell
tobacco containing more than 35 per cent of water."
The Chancellor hoped by this means, " as in the case of
beer, for an increased yield of duty, because more
tobacco would be smoked."

On the Bill becoming law, a month was allowed for
reducing stock, and a further month given up to 21st
July, before the clause was put in operation, in order
to enable manufacturers and retailers to sell off the
tobacco which had been imported at the higher rate of
duty.   On 29th July, 1887, the Excise General Order
was issued to the officers, announcing the new law and
giving instructions to sample, and the administration
of the Moisture Act commenced forthwith.

Many manufacturers, especially those engaged in
keen competition with each other, now endeavoured to
manufacture their goods containing the full statutory
limit of water.   Owing to the unequal distribution of
moisture in tobacco, it happened that some parts of the
finished article contained over 35 per cent, whilst others
contained less.   Timely official warnings failed to stop
the above-mentioned practice, and prosecutions commenced.   Grumblings ensued over the method of
sampling.   Loud cries were made for the taking of a
" fair sample " of their baptized article, whilst it was

TOBACCO WAREHOUSE

affirmed that it was impossible to manufacture a tobacco uniformly containing **35** per cent of moisture. In reply to a complaint of this kind in the House of Commons, Mr. Goschen, while admitting the possibility of the water not being distributed uniformly throughout the tobacco, made it clear that the **35** per cent was intended as a maximum in any portion thereof, and must not be considered as an average.

This Moisture Law has now been in operation for nearly forty years, and although a lot is claimed for its beneficial effects from a revenue point of view, yet from the trade point of view it has proved a veritable thorn in the flesh. The increased price of raw material and the exigencies of competition compel the production of an article containing almost the full statutory limit of moisture. The properties of tobacco, the kinds used and methods of manufacture in making shag and roll, do not permit of an equal distribution of moisture throughout the manufactured article. Especially is this the case with roll tobacco. Consequently there is variation, with an overstepping the statutory moisture limit. Excise officials sample the " loose " stocks of manufacturers weekly, and frequently discover instances of excess moisture. The trade loss and odium arising from frequent prosecutions led manufacturers to interview the Chairman of the Board of Inland Revenue in 1901. Since then only where fraud or continued carelessness have been established, is recourse had to the police court. For accidental infringements of the Moisture Law there is an official system of payment of private fines. Not a year has passed since the institution of this Moisture Act but what has seen batches of manufacturers penalized, sometimes publicly, more often privately, for infringement of this law. The Government Laboratory's annual reports show that for the last ten years the average number of penalties recovered for excess moisture is 15 per cent of the number of manufacturers. This by no means represents the numerous instances of infringement where the manufacturer was simply warned by the Excise authorities—given another chance, so to speak. The official published record of moisture offences proves how difficult it is for manufacturers to carry on their business and comply with the inexorable provisions of this Act. To make matters worse, Sir Michael Hicks Beach, in 1898, altered the moisture limit from 35 per cent to 30 per cent. There was a bitter outcry against this interference, and complaints arose on the part of consumers of their tobaccos being too dry and burning too quickly. Sir Michael, however, gilded the pill by reducing the tobacco duty 4d. per lb. This action left manufacturers three halfpence per lb. to the good, and they made a bit of money in those days.

This state of affairs lasted six years, at the end of which time Sir (then Mr.) Austen Chamberlain put back the limit to 32 per cent, where it now stands. The relief, however, was neutralized by a new duty on stripped tobacco.

Owing to increased price of raw material and, for a time, the adverse influence of fiscal conditions of late years, the smaller manufacturers had found it impossible to produce shag and roll at 3d. an ounce, with the result that the manufacture of this " loose " article had centred in the hands of a few wealthy firms. Not until Mr. Lloyd George's surtax of 8d. per lb. in 1909 had it been found possible to surcharge the consumer. The sum of 8d. per lb. on raw leaf readily permitted of the production of a shag or roll at $3\frac{1}{2}$d. per ounce, containing a maximum 32 per cent of moisture. In this way the manufacturers concerned were able to add three halfpence worth of water per lb. and so partially recoup themselves for the rise in cost of leaf used in producing the poor man's " smoke."

The year 1900 commenced a period of trouble and disquiet to the tobacco trade. The duty reverted to 3s. per lb. Consumption was checked by the financial strain caused by the war and the absence of many smokers in South Africa. Nothing but fiscal and economic troubles have fallen upon the trade since, unless the windfalls in 1902 be excepted to certain retailers, consequent on the lavish generosity of the American Tobacco Trust in the person of Mr. J. B. Duke. Troubles never come singly : 1900 brought the war taxes; 1901 a rise in leaf 2d. per lb., but, fortunately, coal was cheaper. " Invasion " of the American Tobacco Trust and purchase of Ogden's, Ltd., in 1901 and 1902. In 1904 increased duty of 3d. per lb. on stripped tobacco, accompanied by a further rise in price of leaf. 1906, leaf still dearer. 1907 saw crops in the United States held up by planters for increased prices. 1908 brought the prohibition to retailers supplying children under 16 years of age. In 1909-10, Mr. Lloyd George increased the tobacco duty to 3s. 8d. per lb. The South African war, with its scarcity of money, favoured the production of the cheaper priced tobaccos, especially cigarettes. But it discouraged the consumption of dearer smokes, such as cigars. For the last thirty years foreign cigars have been going steadily down, whilst British cigars have gone from worse to worse. In 1900 there were 502 licensed manufacturers, to-day there are but 211. The great majority of those who have dropped out consisted of cigar manufacturers, the smallest, but most numerous, men in the trade. Cigar-making is peculiarly a business that gives proportionately more employment than in any other branch of the tobacco trade, machinery being practically useless here. By the irony of fate, or the want of considerate treatment, the cigar manufacturer has felt the brunt of recent fiscal changes more than any other section of the trade, and it is only since the inquiry of the Tobacco Drawback Departmental Committee, in 1904, that he has been righted in matters of export. Considerations connected with the import duty unduly hit him still and make his lot all the harder to bear. As Cinderella of the trade, the British cigar manufacturer still waits for the Chancellor of the Exchequer to retrieve his position—if by that time there be a position to retrieve.

The " invasion " of the American Tobacco Trust in 1901 struck consternation for a time into the ranks of the tobacco trade. Powerful, rapacious, monopolizing, and unscrupulous, the advent of the Trust president, Mr. J. B. Duke, boded ill for British manufacturers. At first suspense benumbed the trade, then British pluck asserted itself, and thirteen of the principal firms incorporated themselves into the Imperial Tobacco Company, with a capital of £15,000,000, and commenced to fight the alien. The victory lay in the capture of the retailer, and to accomplish this bonuses and baits were showered upon him by both antagonists in bewildering profusion.

The Trust promised a dowry of £200,000 for four years and all Ogden's profits—a promise that the retailers subsequently compelled it to redeem. The Imperial Tobacco Company offered a permanent bonus conditional on the retailers securing certain advertisement privileges to them. Prices were slaughtered. The fight was felt to be one for existence, one or the other was to be annihilated. The British public appreciated the fact that the Imperial Tobacco Company

were battling with the odious Trust principle of " sink
all, that I may swim " and supported the gallant British
platoon.   Thousands of retailers failed to side with Mr.
J. B. Duke and take his gold.   The wary fly refused the
gilt-edged invitation of the decoying spider.   Opposition
proved too strong for the Trust, and ere the summer of
1902 was spent, there came a truce, and, in the end, a
union of forces.   Messrs. Ogden's, Limited, was absorbed
in the British Combine.   The United Kingdom was to be
left alone by the Trust, but with the Combine was to
form a new combination—British-American Tobacco
Company—and acquire the export business of the two.
In contradistinction to the monopolizing policy of a Trust,
the declared policy of the British Combine has been to
" live and let others live." Other manufacturing
firms have since joined, and to-day its output probably
exceeds 75 per cent of the total output of the trade.
The formation and success of the Imperial Tobacco
Company undoubtedly saved not only themselves,
but the firms outside the Combine from the clutches of
the American Trust; but at the same time many of the
smaller manufacturers have but fallen from the frying
pan into the fire.   The formation of the British Combine
has revolutionized trade conditions.   With the continued popularity of its brands, its successful management, and last, but not least, its vast financial resources,
the Combine has progressed and flourished partly
at the expense of smaller firms.   Probably it is
now the largest commercial undertaking in the United
Kingdom.

The Imperial Tobacco Company has endeavoured to
trade fairly.   In some instances prices have been raised
in the teeth of competition and at the risk of loss of
business, rather than produce at a loss.   After all,
there is not a manufacturer living who would not

hesitate to knock out a competitor in fair and open competition. Much as this tendency towards monopoly in the tobacco trade is to be deplored, yet justice compels the admission that on the whole the Combine has refrained from undercutting and hitting rivals below the belt. Its bonus scheme is said to be a weak spot in its armour, yet it is difficult to see how the Imperial can withdraw a promise made to their customers in 1901, viz., a participation in the profits.

Undaunted by past failures in growing tobacco in Ireland, further attempts were made in 1905 and onwards. Legal sanction was given in 1907 to the continuation of these growth experiments, and in the following year an Excise duty of 2s. 10d. per lb. was imposed, being 2d. per lb. less than the Customs duty. This 2d. was not for purposes of protection, but to compensate the owner for the cost of Excise restrictions. By this time Irish planters were producing 68,000 lb. of cured leaf, the assistance of Yankee experts being requisitioned for the purpose. Scotland grew jealous of this Irish success and succeeded in getting the growth benefits extended to that country, especially as the Treasury had granted a rebate of one-third of the Excise duty. By 1909, Ireland had outgrown the experimental stage and so the rebate was commuted to a fixed grant placed at the disposal of the Board of Agriculture to be applied in encouragement of the industry. In the Finance Act of 1909-10, Mr. Lloyd George put the coping stone on this home-growth question by extending permission to England, and so abolishing the old-time prohibition as to commercial culture of tobacco in the United Kingdom.

Just as the South African war tax led to the decline in consumption of higher priced " smokes," so the increase of 8d. per lb. of Mr. Lloyd George's Budget Bill of 1909 led to a further abandonment by consumers of their favourite brands, with the substitution of cheaper and inferior tobaccos. Inasmuch as the cost entailed in popularizing and maintaining these proprietary brands before the public constituted by no means an unimportant item in the goodwill of manufacturers, the effect of Mr. Lloyd George's surtax was disastrous. Manufacturers big and small were placed betwixt the merciless jaws of a closing vice. To escape the inevitable crush manufacturers reverted to the old retail prices existing before the surtax, preferring to incur the monetary loss involved by its payment out of their own pockets, rather than to see the extinction of important branches of their business. This fact does not quite bear out the popular argument that all taxation ultimately falls upon the consumer. With leaf 40 per cent dearer and even 100 per cent in some instances of Turkish varieties, it cannot be said that the lot of the tobacco manufacturer was a particularly happy one. Chancellors of the Exchequer unwittingly helped to drive smokers to the use of commoner tobaccos, and to create a demand for " lugs " and planters' refuse that would in former years have disgraced the offal bag in any tobacco factory.

In 1910 an administrative event occurred that possessed more than an academic interest to the members of the tobacco trade. The Government Laboratory with its two Tobacco Departments—one at the Custom House and the other in the Strand—was cut out of the newly amalgamated Customs and Excise Department, and made to stand on its own base as a separate Government Department.

Speaking numerically, no branch of the tobacco trade is so important as the retailer or distributor. There are 540,519 licensed tobacco dealers in the United

Kingdom, the low licence registration fee of 5s. 3d. favouring the distribution of tobacco. The above number includes publicans, pawnbrokers, grocers, hairdressers and other tradesmen who sell tobacco either as a side line or in addition to their ordinary business, so that it is almost impossible to say how many persons depend solely upon the retailing of tobacco as their means of livelihood.

The distress which covered the world during the years 1914 to 1918 left its marks upon the tobacco industry, although in much less degree than upon some other industries. The very nature of the tobacco trade had something to do with this. Tobacco manufacturers always carry stocks of leaf well ahead of their immediate requirements, so that the leaf may thoroughly mature before being brought into process. Thus it happened that when the war began there was no shortage of the raw material, and it was not until early in 1916 that, in a strictly trade sense, the clouds of war began to hang low over the industry. Until then shipping had been maintained on such a scale that supplies of leaf had been brought in fairly regularly, but the submarine menace became such that some restriction of imports was then necessary. Yet it is worthy of record that the total quantity of tobacco in the bonded warehouses of the United Kingdom on 1st March, 1917, was 112,304 tons (sufficient for two years) in comparison with 104,250 tons on 1st August, 1914. In the Finance Act of September, 1915, the import duty on tobacco was raised by 1s. 10d. per lb., and a further similar increase was proposed by Mr. Bonar Law in his Budget of May, 1917. The second proposal met with a storm of protest and on 16th July following, Mr. Bonar Law adjusted his impost to 50 per cent of his original increase.

The next war measure directly affecting the tobacco industry came on 31st May, 1917, when the Board of Trade made an order under the Defence of the Realm regulations bringing under control all the stocks of manufactured and unmanufactured tobacco and prohibiting the owners of these stocks from dealing with them otherwise than as authorized by the (then constituted) Tobacco Control Board, which had the assistance of an advisory committee consisting of members of the tobacco trade. By the Tobacco Restriction Order the Control Board had absolute authority over the disposal of all tobacco in the country, and from 1st June, 1917, the price of the commodity was fixed at every stage. Owners of tobacco leaf lying in bond were required to make a return of their total stocks in nine days, and rationing of supplies on a basis " not exceeding the deliveries of 1916 " was enforced. The increase in the import duty to 8s. 2d. was estimated to bring to the Treasury £6,000,000 a year, but this sum did not represent the full extra charge to the public, because the manufacturers were compelled to suggest to the Control Board a still higher ratio of retail prices in order to recoup them for the increased charges of manufacture and the additional interest on the money represented in stocks lying in bond. Consideration had also to be given to the increased costs with which distributors, both wholesale and retail, were faced. The Control Board received these representations in a very fair spirit, and although some distributors complained that the new schedule of prices did not give them a sufficient margin of profit, the dissatisfaction was by no means general. Directly opportunity offered, certain adjustments were made in the schedule and the business was thereafter carried on with such satisfaction as the national position permitted. Meantime, the Government had decided to limit the importation of tobacco during the year beginning June, 1917, to 10,000 tons, and at this figure the import remained, approximately, during the rest of the war years. In the year 1916–1917, the total revenue derived by the Treasury from the import of tobacco was £27,375,266.

The assumption of control by the Government led the trade generally to consider anew the question of organization in defence of their own interests. The Imperial Tobacco Company (of Great Britain and Ireland) Limited, was sufficiently powerful to exert its own influence on the Control Board on any question in which it was concerned, but the "independent" manufacturers—that is, those outside the Imperial— were not so powerful, neither were the cigar-making firms. There was already in existence a Tobacco Trade Section of the London Chamber of Commerce which had the active support of a certain number of importers and manufacturers, but the actions of the Government led to a considerable accession of strength to this organization, and eventually sub-sections were formed giving separate representation to the several branches of the industry. Some of the wholesale distributors had previously banded themselves in a Protection Association with members in London and the provinces, and this organization also experienced a large influx of members. In 1907 the Tobacco Trade Travellers' Association had been formed to watch the interests of the " men on the road," and here again there was a large increase in membership.

But the retail distributors, numerically by far the largest section of the trade, had no organization worthy of the name. The necessities of the situation which arose in 1917, however, left them with no alternative but to close their ranks. At a meeting held in London in August, 1917, the National Union of Retail Tobacconists was formed under the presidency of Mr. John Pearson, of Newcastle-on-Tyne (now deceased), a member of the Advisory Committee of the Tobacco Control Board. Branches of the Union were formed in many provincial towns and cities, and the work then undertaken continues to this day, to the increasing benefit of the retail trade. Yet it is true to say that with a return to normal conditions of trade the distributors of tobacco do not, in the main, realize the value of trade organization or they would more quickly swell the ranks of the organization which exists solely for their benefit.

The fundamental steadiness of the industry, which prevented the degree of disturbance by the war experienced by many other trades, likewise accounted for the readiness with which it returned to normal conditions after the great conflict. Tobacco was decontrolled in January, 1919, and very quickly the industry regained its full vitality. It is indeed wonderful the hold which tobacco has upon the human race in general and the British race in particular. It gives one of the largest sources of revenue to the British Government, for in 1935-6 tobacco imported for home consumption totalled the enormous figure of 168,757,383 lb. This figure represents a yearly per capita consumption of nearly 4 lb., but as we are not all smokers the actual consumption by smokers is greatly above the amount indicated. The duty paid on the import of tobacco last year amounted to over £74,000,000 sterling. The figures are dealt with in detail in a later chapter.

CHAPTER II

"TOBACCO flourishes best in regions having a mean temperature of not less than 40° where the early autumn frosts do not nip its aspirations in the bud." The most highly appreciated qualities are, however, developed under the burning sun of the tropics, as in Cuba, Sumatra and the Philippines. There are upwards of forty varieties of the Nicotiana plant, of which only three are in general use by smokers, viz.,

I. *Nicotiana Tabacum*, originally found in America and cultivated extensively there.

II. *Nicotiana Rustica*, grown in Turkey and the Levant, boasts different names : Indian, Syrian, Turkish. It is milder in flavour and makes excellent cigarettes, but burns too quickly for the pipe.

III. *Nicotiana Persica*, Persian tobacco, makes a delicate smoke in a hookah or water pipe, but does not burn well enough to be used in the form of cigars.

[1] For information on this subject I am indebted to the following Works :—
" Cultivation and Curing of Sun-cured Fillers and Wrapper." By Dr. A. J. Fleppo, of Carolina co., V.A.
" Tobacco, from Seed to the Salesroom." By Robert L. Ragland, Halifax co., V.A., Richmond, 1880.
" Instructions how to Grow and Cure Tobacco, especially Fine Yellow." By R. L. Ragland. 1885.
" Tobacco : a Handbook for Planters." By C. G. W. Lock, F.L.S. 1886.
" Tobacco : History and Associations." F. N. Fairholt. 1859 and 1876.
" How Tobacco is Raised and Prepared for the Market." By Southern Fertilizing Co., Richmond, V.A.
" Tobacco Talk." By Nicot Publishing Co. Philadelphia, 1894.
" Tobacco Trade Review," " Tobacco," " Cigar and Tobacco World." Monthly Trade Journals.

To produce the tobacco leaf of commerce requires eighteen months of unremitting labour and attention. The selection and preparation of the soil are important factors in tobacco culture. " The several grades of tobacco, whether for chewing, pipe smoking, or cigars, require different soils and management to ensure a product that will command an adequate return for the labour and means employed on the crop." A cardinal principle in the selection of soil is to obtain one that is porous, well drained, and rich in organic constituents. A wet and tough clayey soil is utterly unsuitable for tobacco farming. Dressings of wood-ashes and other manures are added, and the land is ploughed, rolled, harrowed, etc., it being a proverb with the planter that a " good preparation is half cultivation." Spots sheltered from the wind are chosen for the plants, and in some cases hedges of various kinds are planted to act as wind-screens or canvas cheese-cloth coverings used to prevent the tearing and bruising of the leaves. By the end of March or beginning of April carefully selected seeds are sown in the hot bed or nursery, and in about seven or eight weeks the sturdiest plants are taken on a warm rainy day to the field. Here they are planted in holes made by the finger in the top of hillocks nearly a yard apart, and the farmer's care now commences. Healthy plants are substituted as required for withered and sickly ones ; the soil is constantly heaped up around the plants, continued hoeing is required to remove grass and weeds, and also to loosen the soil. A species of green caterpillar, the " horn-worm," about the size of a man's finger, attacks the plants, eating holes in the leaves and rendering them useless for market, and the destruction of this insect is a duty as incessant as it is imperative. The planter's responsibility increases as the plant thrives. Two

CLEARING THE FOREST FOR TOBACCO IN SUMATRA

months after planting and when from two to seven feet high, flower buds appear, and these are pinched off, or " topped," by experienced and trusty hands in order that the leaves may grow finer and larger. At the same time the top leaves are removed, and also the larger and inferior bottom ones which lie flat and rot, or get dirty and worm-eaten. This latter process is called " priming," it being a general practice to " prime high and top low," but it is not resorted to in all cases of tobacco planting. Only as many leaves are retained on the plant as are likely to mature—from nine to twenty. The constant removal of young suckers is also necessary, the finger nail being used in this " suckering " as in " topping," the nip given by the fingers having the effect of partly closing the wound. During very rainy seasons the plants are subject to a malady called " firing," a kind of blight, and are also seriously affected by the opposite extremes of heat and drought. The plants ripen about three months after being planted, assuming a yellowish green colour, the leaves being occasionally mottled with yellowish spots. They also become gummy, with tips bent downwards. " If there is any dirtier work than raising tobacco," says a planter, " we should like to know it." The resinous exudation from the green leaves smears everything that comes in contact with it.

Harvesting

The ripest plants are selected and cut. Where the stems are thick they are sometimes split from the top to within three inches of the ground, and then cut across near the root and immediately straddled across sticks to prevent their getting bruised. This is the case especially with tobacco known as first " brights." In this manner they are carted to the barn. The ordinary method is simply to cut the stems across and gently lay the plants in rows on one side to wilt in the sun before handling. In some instances the leaves are gathered singly. Too long exposure in the sun produces " sunburn," and hence a cloudy day is selected for the cutting.

DRYING AND CURING

" Growing tobacco," says Lock, " is but half the battle." The most trying time is during the curing process. The methods adopted vary with the description of tobacco harvested, and may be divided into two classes—the " fermentative " and the " non-fermentative " methods. Leaves of a large size, dark and heavy, such as those sent to England and the Continent, and known as " shipping tobacco," are the kinds subjected to the former method, whilst " sun-cured " and " yellow " tobacco are the kinds subjected to the latter. By whatever process tobacco is cured, it must first be dried. To avoid confusion it may be well to describe each method of curing separately, taking first

I.—FERMENTATIVE OR " SWEATING " PROCESS.—The barn or drying house into which the tobacco is placed is not unlike a log-cabin. Across its length inside are stretched tiers of poles, on which are placed slender tobacco sticks with the stalks straddled across them. When the barns are full, fires are started, and the heat is equably distributed by means of flues. The heat is raised to 170° F., and this temperature is retained for four or five days until the leaves become dry and brittle. On a damp day the doors are opened and sufficient moisture is allowed to be absorbed by the leaves to make them pliable, after which they are taken down, stripped from the parent stem, and sorted. The finest and brightest leaves are classed as " firsts " ; slightly inferior ones, of which " shipping tobacco " forms the chief, range as " seconds " ; whilst the worthless and inferior are known as " lugs." The leaves are made up into bundles or " hands," containing from ten to twenty-five leaves, and each class is " bulked " by heaping them together in a pile on the floor. The fermentation process may be said to commence at this stage. The temperature within the heap gradually rises until it reaches 130° F., when the whole mass is pulled to pieces in order to prevent overheating, and the heap is re-formed. Those leaves formerly on the outside of the pile are now placed inside, and by this means uniformity of colour and flavour is attained. In from three to five weeks the leaves assume a uniformly brown tint, and the process is practically complete. The " hands " are occasionally hung upon poles to be entirely " cured." " Tobacco in case " is the term applied to the leaf when it is ready for packing, and moist enough to bear handling without breaking. The leaves then possess a certain elasticity, which is tested by stretching them gently over the ends of fingers and knuckles. " They pull," says Fairholt, " like kid leather, glowing with a kind of moist gloss, not dry enough to break, or damp enough to ferment."

II.—Non-fermentative Process.—This process of curing is performed either by the heat of the sun, producing " sun-cured " or " sun-dried " tobacco, or by the agency of artificial heat in the production of " colory " or " yellow " tobacco.

(a) — " Sun-cured " or " Sun-dried." — Scaffoldings and well-ventilated houses are required, and a temperature of 65° to 75° F., with a certain degree of moisture in the atmosphere, is essential to success. The tobacco plants are placed carefully on a wooden platform,

A FIELD OF RIPE TOBACCO

and by means of planks are prevented from being
wafted by the wind or disturbed in any manner that
would tend to bruise or tear the leaves. The temperature of the air requires careful watching. " A dry hot
sunny day may ' cure ' too fast, not allowing sufficient
time for that rich yellow colour to establish itself which a
slower process of evaporation and desiccation will
produce." Four or five days' sun is sufficient, and the
plants are carefully transferred to a well-ventilated
and well-lighted house. Here they are hung up and
facilities afforded for admitting plenty of light and air,
until the tobacco is perfectly cured, after which the house
is closed. The first four or five days after cutting in a
great measure determine the colour. The earlier, too,
a planter can cut, the better curing weather will be
obtained. Early autumnal frosts are fatal to a tobacco
farm. During winter and spring the tobacco is taken
down when in " soft " order (pliable), and stripped,
bundled, and assorted into " firsts," " seconds," and
" lugs." At the close of each day while stripping,
the several classes are " bulked " or placed together.
If the temperature of the heap rises, the ." hands "
are hung up to dry, and by the end of the spring the
tobacco is ready for the market. This " sun-dried "
article is chiefly sought by manufacturers for making
choice brands of chewing tobacco. " The leaves are
not so large and long as those in ' shipping,' but possess
much finer texture and more strength of fibre. They
are usually of a bright, rich golden brown colour, of a
soft silky feel and appearance, and when properly
prepared for market have a peculiarly sweet odour and
taste, much relished by lovers of the weed." It is
doubtful if much of this " sun-cured " ever finds its
way into England.

(b)—" Colory " Bright Yellow or so-called " Sun-dried."

THE INTERIOR OF A CURING BARN

—" By the process of nature," says Major Ragland, " leaves in dying descend in colour from green through the seven prismatic colours, and finally lose all colour as they go to decay." The cardinal principle in curing fancy yellow tobacco is the employment of a quick dry heat, with the object first to rapidly reach the " yellow " stage of the leaf, and second to fix it. . The heat necessarily must be under complete control—flues of various patterns being used. The first step is known as the " steaming " or yellowing process. An exposure to a temperature of 90° for thirty-six hours is sufficient to turn the leaves yellow. The next step, however, is the important one, viz., fixing the colour. In this process great care is required to prevent the tobacco from " sweating." The first step towards retaining the yellow is to advance the heat to 100° F., to be succeeded by increments of $2\frac{1}{2}$° every two hours, until the most critical point in " fixing " or curing bright tobacco is reached, viz., 110° F. The length of time for which this temperature is retained depends upon the planter's judgment. The period ranges from four to eight hours. When the ends of the leaves begin to curl the heat is increased to 120° or 125° F. At this stage planters state that the curing process sets in. After remaining from four to eight hours, according to the amount of sap to be expelled from the leaf, the heat is raised every hour by 5° up to 170°. Here it remains until stalk and stem are cured. During damp weather the leaves are stripped from the stem, or, if the weather be dry, the tobacco is damped. This is known as the " ordering process." The leaves are assorted, tied into bundles and packed or crowded close together. Again care is necessary to prevent heating and fermentation setting up. After being packed together for some time the tobacco is ready for market.

PRIZING, ETC.

By whatever process tobacco is cured, it is " prized " when removed in large parcels weighing 1,000 lb. and upwards, as in the case of " shipping." This process consists of packing and pressing the " hands " in hogsheads. The latter are regulated in size and structure to a standard, in order that the whole mass of " prized " tobacco can readily be seen and examined. The method of packing is to first place the " hands " or " ties " in a double row across the centre of the hogshead, with the leaves of each row interlocking, so that the butt ends of the " hands " are outwards. Other rows are laid down in a similar manner, smaller " hands " being employed for filling up crevices in order to make the layer even. The layers are alternately placed at right angles to each other until a certain height is reached, when hydraulic pressure is applied to squeeze the whole tightly together. Too great pressure causes blackening of the tobacco, and consequent deterioration in value. During the " prizing " it is stated that in some instances the leaves are " improved " by the addition of sweetening and flavouring matters as, for example, molasses, rum, vanilla, cognac and essential oils. The tobacco seized here in 1876, and which was found to contain small quantities of liquorice and other saccharine matters, had probably been " improved " in the prizing process. Another method of " improving " is to macerate the coarse flavoured leaves in dilute hydrochloric acid, whilst a third method consists in adding solutions of nitrate of potash with the object of imparting a better burning property to the leaf. Whether these statements of planters and others are reliable or not is an open question. Should any " improvements " be discovered in the hogshead on the premises of a tobacco manufacturer in this country, the whole would be forfeited, the tobacco deemed to be " adulterated," and dealt with accordingly.

In " shipping " tobacco a further fermentation sets in after " prizing," which lasts over three weeks, but if the tobacco was in good condition before packing, no apprehension need be felt. It sometimes happens that additional " sweatings " occur during its oceanic journey—some being worthless by the time it reaches its destination.

Large quantities of imported tobacco consist of " strips," i.e. leaves deprived of their midrib, or stalk. The stripping is performed by negroes at stemming factories, the " strips " being tied into bundles, and hung to sweat and dry all through the winter months. By May and in humid weather, the whole is " bulked " and sweated for a fortnight, and subsequently " prized " and shipped.

Before concluding, it may be of interest to draw attention to a class of tobacco different from all others, viz., Latakia. This is a species of tobacco plant grown in the mountainous districts of North Syria, the Laodicea of Scripture, and, contrary to the general practice in cultivation, is allowed to flower. The buds and petals can readily be seen on examination of a sample of cured Latakia. Like Cavalla and Turkish tobacco in general, the leaves are small and delicate—the plants being grown closer together, five inches apart, and from nine to twelve inches between rows. The peculiar dark colour and tarry odour are derived from the method of curing, which consists in exposing the tobacco for six months to the smoke of fires of the Asiatic oak called ozer. (*Quercus Ilex*, or *Quercus Cerris*)

CHAPTER III

THE CHEMICAL CHANGES UNDERGONE IN THE CURING PROCESS

In the works dealing with the subject of tobacco many opinions have been offered as to the chemical changes undergone by the tobacco leaf during the different curing processes employed. No properly conducted experiments appear to have been made on the subject until 1887, when a long and laborious investigation took place on the chemistry of tobacco by Dr. James Bell, the then principal of the Inland Revenue Laboratory, Somerset House, who published the results. The scientific manner in which the subject is treated is beyond the scope and intention of this little work, but it may be pointed out that Dr. Bell showed that the changes undergone in tobacco cured by the " fermentation process " involve, among other things, the decomposition of starch and sugar in the leaves, and the oxidation of the tannin into a dark brown insoluble substance, which determines the colour of the tobacco. In the " non-fermentation process," the starch and sugar produced during growth are preserved. It was found that " topping " induced an accumulation of starch, a small quantity being converted into sugar. The tannin present is also unchanged.

Writing in December, 1911, in *The Cigar and Tobacco World*, Mr. James Scott referred to certain microscopical aspects of curing. A living tobacco leaf contains green (chlorophyll) granules mixed up with yellow ones and starch cells. In curing, the green granules almost disappear and so reveal the yellow ones, whilst at the same time the starch gets converted into gum and sugar.

The rich nitrogenous matter also undergoes changes. " Topping " prevents the starch rising to nourish the flower buds and so causes it to go back to the leaves and stem. The nicotinic principle is first contained in the hair glands—" hair-oil." In curing, the starch, moisture, nitrogenous matter, pass into the midrib, thence into the stalk, " to keep the heart of the plant, as it were, from ' failing.' " The light tinted flecks seen on some leaves during curing are due to the presence of the starch granules. After curing; oxidation with consequent browning of leaves occurs, heat being the arresting agent.

Research work is being undertaken to-day in almost every tobacco-growing country, either by Government departments or by associations interested in the growth or manufacture of the product. Beneficial work in this direction has been done in many parts of the British Empire, for by a study of the product and the changes it undergoes in the various stages of preparation for the market, and of the effect of varying conditions on the cultivation, knowledge is obtained which enables the grower to produce an article which will appeal to the palate of the consumer whose custom he desires. Some of the important directions in which research has given valuable help have been in the combating of disease in the plants, the effects of manuring, improvements in quality and aroma of the leaf, curing and grading, and in improving the strains.

CHAPTER IV

IN BOND

UNMANUFACTURED tobacco for pipe and cigarette smoking comes into the United Kingdom in huge wooden casks called hogsheads. Cigar and Turkish leaf come in bales. The old standard weight of a hogshead is 1,000 lb. ; the bales vary in weight, being about 120 lb. more or less. Nearly all raw tobacco imported in bulk is warehoused, the proprietor giving bond for the due security of the duty. In other words, he stands bail to the Crown for the tobacco in his bonded warehouse, and is responsible for the duty should any hogshead or bale be missing. Manufactured tobaccos come in cases. A case of cigars may contain 100 boxes, i.e. about 10,000 cigars. Temperature and dryness of a bonded warehouse have to be carefully considered. Tobaccos require frequent examination and attention, especially those in bales, and much depends on the experience, judgment and care of the warehouse-keeper. The bonded warehouse is the trade store : it is also the Government toll-house.

The middleman who buys from the planter and sells to the manufacturer is called a tobacco broker ; the middleman who buys cigars, etc., from foreign manufacturers and imports them, is known as an " importer." Of late years brokers have had a bad time owing to the practice of " big " manufacturers acting as their own brokers ; the importers, too, have suffered owing to decreased consumption of their goods. There is always a two years' reserve stock kept in bond—a necessary precaution nowadays—and as the Customs duty is not paid until the tobacco is delivered, the merchant is saved the additional outlay of capital. A stock of over 350,000,000 lb. of duty-free tobacco entails great responsibility on the warehouse keeper and on the custodians of the revenue.

The purchase of this huge amount of tobacco in advance, together with the loss of interest on the money expended and payment of warehouse rent, constitute an additional tax on the manufacturer.

To the Crown this gigantic bulk represents about £140,000,000 in the form of duty. Hence, the jealous care and close control exercised by the Customs Department in collecting the tax. These bonded warehouses are scattered all over the United Kingdom in places convenient to the tobacco merchants. As so much depends on the structural security of the building, the Customs prescribe the construction of each warehouse and place a Crown lock on the door. The official regulations governing the warehousing of tobacco, constitute a code of intricate laws that require time and experience to master. Apart from weighing and assessing duty, a lot of operations are conducted in bond—re-packing, drying, garbling, blending, butting, sampling, manufacturing, checking, examining, transferring, repairing, and destroying refuse in the warehouse furnace—the only kind of " King's pipe " now in vogue. In weighing hogsheads for duty, the head is knocked off and the cask is turned upside down on to the scales, when the wooden casing is removed, so that only the net tobacco is weighed. It is then replaced in its wooden casing. Bale tobacco is weighed, either net or a tare allowed for the covering.

When unmanufactured tobacco is cleared from warehouse to the factory an official " permit " is sent with it to prove that it is " duty-paid." In the absence of this important document of the Crown, the Excise officer in charge of the tobacco factory would seize the hogshead and there would be trouble for the manufacturer.

CHAPTER V

BRITISH CIGARS

THE earliest form of Tobacco Smoking is probably in a pipe, although some form of a cigar has been known from early times.

The primitive cigars would be merely a few leaves of tobacco loosely rolled up in the hand, and one end of the roll inserted in the mouth, the other being lit. From this the commercial Cheroot would soon be evolved and a gradual but continuous endeavour to improve the appearance of the cigar has resulted in the numerous attractive shapes now on the market.

There seems to be no evidence of cigar manufacturing in England prior to the nineteenth century, and the trade was but a small one until about 1840, when a rapid increase in the production took place, and the industry began to flourish, so that by 1851 several British cigar manufacturers were included in the list of exhibitors in the great exhibition.

Until about 1860 most of the cigars made were of a straight shape, but a " bellied " cigar then came into favour and to facilitate the production of this class of goods a wooden " mould " or " form " was invented to press the fillers into any desired shape before the wrapper was applied.

From this date cigars were divided into two classes—the " hand-made cigar " and the one fashioned with the aid of the " mould " " mould-made."

The expert maker soon learned to produce any desired shape without the aid of the mould, and a hand-made cigar usually smoking more evenly and freely than the other variety, the moulds were retained as a help to the less expert makers in producing an attractively shaped cigar at a low price.

From time to time attempts have been made to introduce machinery into the cigar trade, but although a considerable number of cheap cigars are made wholly or in part by machinery, they are unable to compete with cigars made by an expert hand maker.

Cigars were usually packed into cedar boxes of 100 or " tenths " (being sold at so much per 1,000); at a later date boxes of 50's. and 25's. ($\frac{1}{20}$ and $\frac{1}{40}$) were introduced and are now the general form of packing.

At first the only ornamentation on the box was the name of the cigar branded in the box lid as a trade mark. Some dealers had an impression of the brand printed on plain or coloured paper and stuck inside the box lid, and from this origin has grown the " labelling " of a cigar box with the finest specimens of the chromo lithographer's art.

The difficulty of identifying a cigar away from its box led to some manufacturers gumming a small " ticket " or star of coloured paper with the name of the brand on each cigar, but as it was found difficult to remove these " tickets " without damaging the cigar, or to smoke the cigar beyond the " ticket " without spoiling the flavour, the " ticket " was replaced by a paper " ring " or " band " as now used. During the last few years a fashion has been established to do away with all labels and bands on cigars and to pack them in cedar cabinet boxes, a method of packing which certainly conduces to preserving the original flavour of the cigar unimpaired.

Some of these cabinets now on sale are most ornate and expensive, and range in size from one containing but 50 cigars to one containing 10,000.

As the origin of the cigar was in the Spanish West

PACKING AND FORWARDING

Indies it was customary to mark all cigars with Spanish names, and prior to the passing of the Trade Marks Act, 1875, boxes were so branded and labelled that it was impossible for the public to distinguish a British or Continental cigar from one made in Cuba—in fact they were all branded " Havana " !

After this date the word " Havana " was removed from British cigars, but the use of the Spanish words, etc., continued without opposition until 1907, when an Association of Cuban Manufacturers and Importers was formed to protect the Cuban cigar from imitation, and to seek to compel makers of and dealers in non-Havana cigars to cease using Spanish words or pictures on their cigar boxes.

This campaign met with a considerable measure of success, a number of convictions being obtained against tobacconists who were selling cigars under labels and brands so closely imitating the Cuban style of packing as to be calculated to deceive the public.

As, however, the use of Spanish words on cigars is so universal, the courts have held that the mere use of a Spanish brand name on a box of cigars is not illegal, and that by general custom the use of Spanish words denoting colour, shape and size is quite unobjectionable.

During the many years in which cigars have been made in this country, a number of new growths of tobacco have been brought into use.

At first cigar manufacturers drew all their supplies from the West Indies and the adjacent Mainland of Central and South America. Then tobacco was received from the Philippine Islands (Manila). After this many of the islands of the Malay Archipelago were brought under Tobacco Cultivation—in succession Java, Sumatra and Borneo yielded good crops of tobacco suitable for cigars, and now much of the very highest priced wrapper tobacco is obtained from the East Indies ; whilst cigar tobacco of inferior grades is obtained from India, Japan, South Africa, Germany, Holland, Russia and Hungary, as well as the United Kingdom.

All cigar tobaccos are leaves from local varieties of the plant *Nicotiana Tabacum*, which grows luxuriantly in all tropical and sub-tropical climates.

The seedling plants are transplanted into a good rich soil, either virgin or well manured, and carefully tended until the leaves are ripe for cutting.

After cutting the leaves are strung up to dry, and are then placed in large heaps to ferment. This fermentation requires expert guidance as, on it, the flavour, appearance and value of the tobacco depend.

After fermentation the tobacco is again dried and then packed into bales for shipment to any place where it may be required.

On landing in England the packages are weighed net and stored in Bonded Warehouses until required by the manufacturer. He pays duty on the raw tobacco, which is then delivered into his factory.

The first process is to damp the tobacco to make it pliable so that the midrib or " stalk " can easily be " stripped " from the leaf ; these stalks can be used for snuff. After the stalks are removed the tobacco is graded into "Wrappers" or "Binders," "Bunch Wrappers," and "Fillers." The fine perfect leaves of good appearance and free burning, the "Wrappers," are used for the outer cover of the cigars ; leaves less perfect in appearance, etc., are used as "Bunch Wrappers" or "Binders" around the smaller leaves and broken pieces which are used to make up the inside of the cigars as "Fillers."

The cigar makers sit at tables of a convenient height, the appliances used being a hard wood board on which tobacco can be cut to shape and the cigars rolled ; a knife to cut the wrappers ; a pair of scissors to trim leaf and a cutter gauge to cut off the lighting end of a cigar straight across at any desired distance from the point, so as to make all cigars of the same kind exactly the same length.

The maker places in his left hand a number of pieces of " filler " tobacco, so arranged as to produce roughly the desired length, thickness and shape of the cigar he is making, he then places this tobacco on a piece of " bunch wrapper " of the desired size, and rolls up the fillers into a " bunch " or roll which now requires the addition of the wrapper to be a finished cigar.

This bunch is placed on one side whilst the wrapper is cut, and this requires great care on the part of the operative who has to bear in mind not only the shape of the cigar he is to make, but the characteristics of the tobacco he is using, and any small faults such as holes, etc., it may contain.

The wrapper has to be cut of such a shape as will wrap closely around the cigar, and in such a way that the side veins in the leaf will run straight up and down the cigar—a vein running round the cigar in a spiral is not pretty.

As a tobacco leaf is thinner and finer towards its edges, each side of a leaf has to be so cut and used that the edge is on top when wrapped on the cigar, and that the thicker part of this leaf is underneath, the " top " side of the leaf has also to be outside, so that the left-hand side of a tobacco leaf has to be rolled in quite a different way from the other side—in fact, one side is rolled with the maker's left hand, and the other with his right hand.

When the wrapper has been rolled around the cigar, commencing at the lighting end (or " tuck " as it is called in a shaped cigar) it is necessary to finish the point

By permission of   Messrs. Martin, Ltd.

CIGAR MAKING

so as to prevent the cover unwrapping. This point is gummed down with a tasteless and colourless gum, usually gum tragacanth ; this little touch of gum being the only matter that is not pure tobacco which enters into the composition of a cigar.

In making a " moulded " cigar the operative rolls a bunch in the same way, but to obtain the desired shape it is laid in one of the shaped recesses of the " mould " and then pressed into shape ; when the bunch so shaped is " set," it is taken out of the mould and covered with the wrapper in the usual way.

In most moulded cigars two long ridges or marks appear, one on each side, running the whole length of the cigar ; these are produced by the bunch wrapper being slightly trapped between the two sections of the mould when they are pressed together.

To obviate these marks the " bunches " are sometimes unrolled and the " mould mark " smoothed out, but the extra cost of doing this takes away from the saving as compared with hand work.

When the maker has made 100 cigars they are sent to the foreman who has them examined for faults of workmanship, and after any faulty cigars have been thrown out, they are placed in a box until a considerable number of cigars of the same quality, size and shape have accumulated, when they are given to the " sorter " whose duty it is to grade them as to colour, and then to box them, either loose or in bundles tied up with ribbon.

After the cigars have been sorted into a number of heaps, from the lightest to the darkest, the sorter picks out twelve or thirteen cigars of precisely the same shade, and each cigar as perfect as possible—these cigars form the " face " or top layer of a box. The other rows are first put into the box and pressed down, and finally the specially selected top row is put in.

DRYING-ROOM FILLERS

By permission of

Messrs. Martin, Ltd.

In a box of **50** there are usually two rows of **12** and two of **13**, thus :—

$$
\begin{array}{ccc}
12 & \text{or} & 13 \\
\overline{} & & \overline{} \\
13 & & 12 \\
\overline{} & & \overline{} \\
12 & & 13 \\
\overline{} & & \overline{} \\
13 & & 12
\end{array}
$$

a " square " box has five rows of ten.

A box of 25 has one 12 and one 13, or if square 8—9—8.

A box of 100 has usually four rows each of 12 and 13, but in some cases has four rows of 16 and two of 17, and some long boxes have five rows of 20.

Bundled cigars are tied up with silk ribbon (usually yellow in colour) either 100, 50, 25, or 10 in a bundle.

The boxes are usually of a fine cedar wood, but cheap boxes are made of mahogany, and in some cases of alder wood.

After boxing, the full boxes are placed in a press so that the lids are pressed down to give the top layer of cigars a smooth appearance, and then left to dry either slowly and naturally, or they are placed in a room artificially warmed if they are required in a hurry.

When in condition all that remains to be done is to paste or glue on the outside labels, and with a stencil brush mark the colours, etc., on the box, " claro " being cigars of the lightest shade, " colorado claro," " colorado," " colorado maduro," on to " maduro," which is the darkest.

A perfect cigar should appeal in a pleasant way to the senses of taste, smell and sight ; it should be well made, of an attractive shape, it should burn freely and evenly, with an agreeable flavour and a fine aroma.

By permission of

Messrs. Martin, Ltd.

FILLERS BLENDING

The public demand at present runs in favour of a fine light silky wrapper burning with a white ash, it being thought that such a cigar must be of mild flavour.

As a matter of fact, a light coloured wrapper is little, if any, indication of the strength of the cigar, as a fine silky wrapper will not exceed a twentieth of the entire weight of the cigar, and the fillers may be quite full flavoured.

Other things being equal, a well matured leaf of medium colour is better in flavour than the extremely light ones, which—being probably somewhat unripe and under-fermented—are often bitter.

To produce the fine, thin silky leaves so much in fashion, a considerable quantity of tobacco is grown under the shade of a cheesecloth covering, and such tobacco is deprived of the full benefit of the sun's rays, and cannot compare in quality and aroma with one grown under natural conditions.

Some of the finest light wrappers are grown in Sumatra and Borneo, where the climate and soil are more suitable for the growth of thin tobacco of but mild flavour, whereas the West Indian tobacco, though not so smooth, has its flavour more developed.

The finest quality of tobacco for cigar purposes is grown in the Vuelto Abajo district of Cuba, not far from the city of Havana, and cigars made from this class of tobacco have always commanded the highest possible price.

With tobacco of equal quality and given equal ability in the workpeople and blenders, cigars can be produced as well in one country as another; but as the best tobacco is grown in Cuba, and the cigars made in Havana have earned a very great reputation and commanded the highest prices, the Cuban manufacturer is able to

By permission of

STRIPPING AND PADDING LEAF TOBACCO

outbid his competitors for the best tobacco, and the very finest cigars are made in and around Havana.

Of late years a marked improvement in the quality of British made cigars has taken place, and, undoubtedly, at any price within the reach of the ordinary smoker the British made cigar is now supreme.

CHAPTER VI

CUT TOBACCO

UNDER the term "cut tobacco" will be included in this chapter the various kinds of tobacco which are manufactured and sold in a form ready for use in a pipe or for making into cigarettes by the consumer, the only treatment required for use being, in the case of some cut-flake or bar tobacco, to rub it between the hands in order to loosen the compressed state in which it leaves the cutting machine and is packed for sale.

It may be premised here that the first stage in the manufacture of all kinds of tobacco is practically the same. Tobacco, as imported, is tightly packed in hogsheads or bales, the leaves being fastened together into small bundles or "hands" by means of a tobacco leaf twisted round the base of the leaves. In this state the tobacco is too dry and brittle for manufacture, containing only 12 to 15 per cent of moisture. The "hands" are undone and passed through steam-heated chambers at a temperature of 120° to 160° F., and if the stalk or midrib has not been removed before importation, it is now stripped from the leaf. The stripped leaves are then left in heaps or "beds" for the added moisture to impregnate it and render the leaves supple and workable, these heaps being left for twenty-four hours. At this stage the manufacturer usually sprays over it any flavouring or perfume which he desires the finished article to possess. It is an open question whether the average consumer has any particular fondness for a scented tobacco, but the use of a flavouring, the composition of which is known only to the manufacturer,

63

enables any particular brand which, from its popularity, might otherwise be liable to imitation or counterfeit to be ear-marked, so to speak, and easily identified.

The elementary, and probably the original, way of manufacturing cut tobacco is, or was, then to pass the leaf through a cutting machine. This, in all but small and minor operations, contains a mechanically driven knife working rapidly *à la* guillotine, and capable of being set or gauged to cut the leaf coarse or fine according to requirements.

The cut leaf, in which the moisture is somewhat in excess, is then panned or stoved, i.e. it is spread out on hot metal plates and, while on them, continually turned to prevent scorching. Considerable art is displayed by the operator at this stage, as during the panning the moisture is reduced to the requisite extent and the aroma of the tobacco developed. After panning, the tobacco is spread out thinly on trays, placed in tiers, where it cools down to the temperature of the air.

At the present time, most imported tobacco leaf pays a duty of 9s. 6d. per lb., and as the retail price of the cheap forms of tobacco is 1s. per oz. or 16s. per lb. (excluding "Preference" Tobacco), much of the manufacturer's and retailer's profit is derived from the moisture imparted during manufacture. The legal limit of moisture is 32 per cent, and competition therefore prompts the trade to aim as near as safety allows at this proportion.

After the cut tobacco has cooled, manufacturers who work on a large scale make analytical tests of each batch to ensure that the legal limit is not exceeded. Modern competition and fashion have produced varieties of cut tobacco which require more complicated methods of manufacture. In order to produce the compact forms of flake, etc., the leaf from the "beds" is placed in a box press which can be subjected to hydraulic pressure, from which it emerges as a hard slab about 1½ inches thick. These slabs are cut into bars, and the bars are wrapped by hand with good sound leaf and again pressed. This wrapping produces on the pressed bars a smooth face which is not disturbed in the process of cutting, which cuts the bars into thin sections or " flakes "—hence the grained or mottled appearance of flakes which are packed in boxes or tins without being rubbed up.

Dark shags are produced by moulding the loose leaf into slabs or blocks and then subjecting them to a slight baking before cutting.

Cut Cavendish and similar descriptions of black cut tobacco known by various local names, such as Chester Shag, etc., are manufactured in a similar manner, the process of baking or stoving being more prolonged ; and in some cases, the iron plates between which the blocks are pressed are smeared with olive oil, which assists the blackening.

Bird's-eye tobacco owes its name to the inclusion with the leaf of a proportion of stalk, the fine sections of which have a fancied resemblance to a bird's eye. Until recent years, bird's-eye was, as a rule, a comparatively high-class tobacco, but the small extra duty now levied on stripped leaf has caused much larger quantities of whole leaf to be imported, with the result that stalks are now rather too plentiful for the tobacco manufacturer's purpose, and in consequence, cheap bird's-eye at the minimum price is now on the market.

The variety known as " Returns " was formerly a fine cut pale yellow American leaf, well adapted for the consumer who made his own cigarettes. Recent increased taxation and competition have, however, produced cheaper kinds of " Returns," containing an admixture of China or Greek leaf, both of which are more easily combustible, but much inferior to American leaf.

Smoking mixtures generally contain a proportion of Perique or Latakia, or both ; Perique is considered the strongest tobacco of all. It is grown in Louisiana, and to a very small extent. It is an almost black, very moist leaf, as imported, and is grown in damp, marshy land. Latakia is grown in Asia Minor and is a small variety of the tobacco plant, being only a few inches in length. In manufacture, the whole plant above ground is employed. Its characteristic flavour is said to be due to the fuel—dried camel dung—used in curing it. Both it and Perique are too strong to be used alone ; indeed, a pipeful of either would produce for the average seasoned smoker all the symptoms of a youth's first cigar.

CHAPTER VII

THESE varieties of manufactured tobacco are stronger in flavour than most cut tobaccos. As sold, they are adaptable for chewing, and thus are a useful solace to the consumer who, for reasons of safety or discipline, is precluded from enjoying a smoke. In order to smoke them they require to be cut and rubbed up.

Roll, twist, pigtail, etc., are manufactured in the following manner : the leaf having been already liquored and rendered pliable, is sorted by separating the largest and sound leaves from the torn or broken ones. These become, respectively, wrappers and fillers. They are next converted by the operatives into coils or ropes with the aid, generally, of a spinning machine, the fillers forming the inside, and the wrappers the outside of the coil. As the coil leaves the hands of the workers it is drawn into the machine, which imparts to it a spiral motion, and as far as possible a smooth, unbroken surface, and coils it on a reel. At this, the spinning stage, olive oil is used on the leaf if it is intended that the finished article shall be black. The art of the spinner consists in producing a spun coil of uniform diameter. This varies from $\frac{1}{4}$ inch or less for thin pigtail up to that of the thickest roll, which may be about two inches. The reels are next conveyed to other workers who prepare the spun leaf for the press. If it is intended to make nailrod or any other straight form of hard tobacco, the coil is simply cut into lengths which are packed in parallel, in box presses, oiled paper being placed between the layers to prevent them from sticking together, so that when ready for sale they can be separated without tearing the wrapper or face.

If Roll is to be made, the operative, with the aid of a small hand machine, coils the spun leaf spirally to the extent required by the intended thickness of the roll. Another layer is then wound over this, and so on, increasing the diameter of the roll till the final size and weight are attained. These rolls vary from pigtails at 1 lb. up to rolls of about 30 lb. The coils or layers are held together with strips of bass and wooden pegs, and each layer is brushed or rubbed with olive oil to prevent sticking. When the required size is reached, the roll is wrapped in canvas, and tightly and closely bound round with stout cord to prevent bursting.

" Target " is made by coiling the spun tobacco into one layer, each target being separated from the next by a layer of oiled paper or canvas, and an iron plate, for the baking and pressing stages.

The rolls, etc., are next baked for a few hours, after which they are placed in strong presses where they remain for a few days or perhaps two or three weeks, according to demand. Oil, heat and pressure are the three factors which, jointly, have the greatest effect in producing a good black, hard roll, with a nice glossy surface. If blackness is not required, oil or heat, or both are omitted. Thus, pressed brown roll may be merely pressed after making up, while what is known as " Newcastle Brown " is simply coiled (spun) and pegged into spherical rolls and sold in the same condition as when spun.

Other forms of hard tobacco are plug, bar, cake, etc. These are made by moulding loose leaf in metal frames, subjecting it to hydraulic pressure, facing the block with sound leaf and again pressing ; or the facing is performed on sections produced by cutting larger blocks of pressed leaf into the required size and shape. Sometimes the final pressing is carried out with metal plates which impress the name of the brand on the finished article.

CHAPTER VIII

IT is a fact that, in recent years, with the enormous increase in the number of cigarettes consumed, the number made by consumers themselves has greatly diminished. This is undoubtedly due to the advent of the cigarette-making machine.

The machine to a great extent has displaced hand-made cigarettes, and it has popularized cigarettes among classes who formerly did not smoke at all, or, if they did, used the pipe, e.g. women, adolescents and working men.

Most of the tobacco used in cigarettes is light Virginia leaf of various qualities.

The process of manufacture is the simplest one in the trade. The leaf, having been slightly damped to render it pliable, is stripped of its stalk or midrib in the case of American leaf (Turkish leaf is too small to need stripping) and is passed through a cutting machine set to cut it fine. The cut tobacco is then passed through steam-heated rotary cylinders to remove excessive moisture and bring out its aroma. Particular care is required in this operation to obtain an even moisture content. The "rag," as it is termed, passes on to a rotary cooler, where the sand and dust are also removed. It is then matured for three days before being fed into the cigarette-making machine.

In making hand-made cigarettes, the paper, contrary to the method of the amateur maker or consumer, is rolled, and the edge stuck down or crimped, before it is filled with tobacco. The operative rolls the tobacco in a small piece of parchment, inserts the end of the rolled parchment in the end of the prepared paper sheath, or "spill," as it is termed in the trade, and

69

pushes the tobacco from one into the other with a pencil-shaped stick. This gives the cigarette a little too much tobacco, the excess protruding at each end being cut off with scissors. If the cigarette is to be tipped with cork or gold leaf, the tip has to be stuck on afterwards by hand also, so that it can easily be imagined what deftness of hands and fingers the makers possess. The spills are of course made beforehand in quantity, either by hand or by a machine. or in some cases. obtained ready-made from the paper makers.

A full description of the modern electrically driven cigarette-making machine, used to-day in practically every factory in the country, would be too technical and involved for a book of this size and nature; so a very brief summary of its principal features will have to suffice.

The paper for the covering of the cigarette is obtained rolled in discs about a foot in diameter, the thickness, or width of the paper strip, being slightly more than the circumference of a cigarette. As this strip is unrolled from the disc and proceeds to the machine a printing mechanism automatically prints the name, etc., on the paper, the printing device being so geared with the machine that the imprint is always in the middle or towards the end of the cigarette, whichever is desired. The strip of paper entering the machine is met by the tobacco, which has been fed into hoppers from which it travels automatically on its journey, and the paper is rolled lengthways around the tobacco and stuck down at the edge, thus forming a continuous cigarette. If this cigarette was not cut until all the paper had been run off the disc it would be a mile long, for that is about the length of the strip. However, as the paper and tobacco are fed in at one end of the machine, the continuous tube is met at the other end by revolving knives which cut it into even lengths, and the cigarettes are then complete.

The amazing speed at which these operations are carried out may be imagined from the fact that the latest machines turn out anything from 800 to 1000 finished cigarettes a minute; and the processes are so mechanized and automatic that only one attendant is necessary to five or six machines.

The tobacco naturally has to be in a "workable" condition for the cigarette-making process, so for twenty-four hours after making the cigarettes are dried or "conditioned," poorly-fashioned ones being sorted out by an expert staff.

These imperfect cigarettes, and the first and last few feet of cigarette made from a complete strip of paper, pass through a special machine which separates the tobacco from the paper, and the tobacco then can be used again.

The cigarette-making machine is only one of the numerous machines used in a factory. To mention just two or three there are the machines for making the cardboard containers and filling them with cigarettes; another machine for making the paper containers used for certain makes of cigarettes packed in fives; and, where hand-made cigarettes are made, there is a machine for making the "spills."

CHAPTER IX

THE TURKISH CIGARETTE

THERE are comparatively few spots on this globe where Nature has put forth her very best efforts to grow tobacco, and one of these favoured sun-kissed places is the land of the peach and plum. Just as the Vuelto-Abajo produces the world-renowned tobacco for the cigar, so the mountainous districts of Macedonia bring forth the richly-prized tobacco for the cigarette. Professors may talk, chemists may test, farmers may plant, but no tobacco ever can be grown that is equal to the modest little plant culled by the peasants of the Levant. It is a desideratum that in all tobacco culture there must be a happy conjunction of natural circumstances in the workshop of Nature to produce the finest product. The failure of one of these dovetailing forces simply means missing the acme of perfection as surely as the tiniest speck on the petal impeaches the absolute beauty of the rose. Too much or little sun at the eventful moment, an adventitious shower or inopportune wind bruising the delicate tissues of a highly-matured plant, a capricious variation of atmospheric conditions just sufficient to prevent the unfolding of the fullest luxuriance of the aromatic herb—these are factors against which man can but pray, but whose absence results in an unimpeachable faultlessness and success. Such Turkish tobacco in its purity, fragrance and sweetness, possesses that subtle and delicious aroma that places it like a god amongst men. Cigarettes made of this enchanting herb have no rival. They stand on the topmost pinnacle —incomparable and alone.

In this word-painting of the excellence of the Turkish cigarette it is an outrage on taste to smirch beauty by reference to commoner kinds. Hence the foregoing paragraph is left on its own easel, and a second commenced with some clouds on the horizon to give warning to the heedful that the sky has its clouds and the sea its phases. There is an old familiar adage that " All is not gold that glitters," and the same is true of tobacco grown in Turkey. There is Turkish tobacco and Turkish tobacco, and there is as much difference between the two as there is between the noble and the peasant. Tobacco differs like children, and until these children are brought into one family circle, they will continue to exhibit the different characteristics habitual to each individual. In other words, the Turkish leaf requires to be mixed and blended before the ideal Turkish cigarette can be produced. There are some children too wayward and uncouth for any teacher to train, and there are some varieties of tobacco grown in Turkey that would disgrace a dunghill. To select the good from the bad, to discriminate between the characteristics of leaf on this farm and leaf on that, to know the indigenous flavour of the plant when grown on this slope and when planted on that flat—and to blend so as to produce the desired aroma, just as a statistician can cast a sum—these are niceties requiring personal supervision and long-trained expert experience. There may be said to be three varieties of Turkish tobacco :—North Asia Minor (Samsoun and Trebizonde districts), South Asia Minor (Smyrna Ayoussolouk varieties), Turkey in Europe (Macedonian-Yenidjeh, Cavalla, etc.).

Of the cigarette leaf the best qualities come from Mahalla, in Macedonia, and are shipped from Cavalla, the port of Macedonia. Another fine cigarette leaf comes from Samsoun, on the Black Sea. Below these in quality is the leaf from Thessaly, Greece, Bosnia, Serbia, Rumania, the Crimea, and the Caucasus. When the best grade of leaf is assorted and the imperfect ones thrown out, that which remains is known as Dubec, a word often used incorrectly by most people to indicate a place instead of a quality or selection.

Cavalla varieties are packed by placing the leaves together very much as cards are placed in a pack, only those of the same length being employed in the same layer. As the finest leaf is the top one on the stalk, and therefore the smallest, this length becomes a basis of classification. Six lengths are recognized, which give just so many classes.

The Samsoun leaf is packed in little bundles of twelve and fifteen, which are fastened together, and these bundles form the units of the layer. In the after process of packing, the two grades follow the same course. With the Cavalla the packed leaves are assembled with their stems vertical, and are formed into an elliptical layer about 2 feet long and 5 inches in diameter. This makes the depth—which is, of course, the length of the leaf—2 inches. With the Samsoun variety the little bundles are brought together in the same way, and are formed into a similar ellipse, but considerably deeper than the Cavalla. The result of this is seen in inspecting the leaf. When opening a bale of Cavalla and separating a layer, each leaf may be removed separately without disturbing the rest ; but with the Samsoun, the layer breaks into the little bundles of twelve or fifteen already described.

In flat bales, made up of parallel layers, the tobacco reaches London. Large quantities go to Egypt to be made into " Egyptian " cigarettes. To the inexpert eye all the bales seem about the same ; but if they were made into cigarettes without any further treatment the result would be startling. Some would burn well, and others badly ; some would be flat and insipid, others too aromatic ; some would have no effect upon the smoker, while others would act as a nervine. Here comes in the skill of the blender. With trained eye and nostril, he recognizes the quality of each leaf and makes a mixture of several varieties, which gives a perfectly uniform cigarette.

It has already been remarked that the finest leaf is the top one on the stalk, and no one knows this better than the peasants employed on tobacco farms and warehouses in Macedonia. If not carefully supervised these leaves will be abstracted for " home consumption "; special watch has to be maintained to prevent what would otherwise be an irreparable loss. Throughout the big hotels and shops of London and the provinces the English-made Turkish cigarettes are noted, and many of the hotels on the Continent, despite the high tariffs erected against these luxuries, will have no other kind.

The leaves being so small there is no need to deprive them of their midribs. They are cut either by hand or by machinery. Hand labour is a distinctive feature in the making of Turkish cigarettes. The blending process is an interesting sight : the operator selects handfuls from baskets containing the various kinds of leaf and showers them on to the floor in order to secure as thorough a mixture as is possible. A slight quantity of water is sprinkled upon the mass of fallen leaves, just sufficient to produce pliability and the heap is left all night. By the following morning the dry leaves have absorbed the water sprinkling, and so become pliable, and the whole is ready for the cutting machine. No heat is employed as in the case of Virginian tobacco, otherwise the delicate aroma of a Turkish leaf would be lost. The method of manufacture follows that already given under Virginian cigarettes. In 1910, the quantity of leaf imported from Turkey was 4,500,000 lb.

CHAPTER X

CAVENDISH AND NEGROHEAD

THERE are two kinds of tobacco manufactories, viz., Excise factories and Bonded factories. In the former, only tobacco on which duty has been paid is allowed to be manufactured, and the premises are subject to Excise survey and restrictions. In the latter, tobacco is received duty-free, and duty is only paid on the manufactured goods sent out for home consumption. Bonded warehouses are usually under Customs supervision, and officers are constantly in attendance while manufacturing operations are in progress. When the officers leave they secure the warehouse with Revenue locks.

A bonded warehouse in which Cavendish or Negrohead is manufactured must be constructed strictly in accordance with the requirements of the warehousing code. It must be built of stone, brick, or concrete, and the windows must be secured by iron bars, fixed at regular intervals outside, and strongly embedded in the stone or brick work. Doors must be strongly built, and so fixed that they cannot be lifted from their hinges. Gauze must be fixed over windows required to be open for ventilation, shutters must be provided to certain windows, and chimneys must be secured by iron bars placed across them. Further, the bonded manufacturer must give bond to the Crown in a sum sufficient to cover any loss by robbery or fraud; proper office accommodation for the Revenue officials must be provided, and the bonded warehouse must be approved by the Board of Customs and Excise before it can be used.

The original Act allowing the manufacture of tobacco in bond is the Manufactured Tobacco Act, 1863, applying to Customs warehouses, and this was extended by the Revenue Act, 1898, to Excise warehouses. The former Act was one of Mr. Gladstone's legislative achievements, and simple though it may seem, it clearly draws a line between tobacco manufactured in bonded warehouses duty-free, and that manufactured in Excise factories, by the simple expedient of adding sugar to that made in bond. This sweetening matter is added to the tobacco in the form of a solution, but only a very small percentage is required. All tobacco so treated is termed Cavendish or Negrohead, whatever it may be, be it cigars, cigarettes, cake or cut tobacco. It is interesting to note here that Cavendish is so named after the great admiral of that name of the time of Queen Elizabeth. He first devised sweetened tobacco, and introduced it into this country.

The casual visitor to a bonded tobacco factory would soon note the difference from an Excise tobacco factory. He would observe the officers in attendance, the secure manner in which the warehouse is built, and he would further note the duty compartment, and the place provided for storing the spirits and sugar used in manufacture. This duty compartment is built from the warehouse floor to the ceiling, and is like a warehouse within a warehouse. Any Cavendish intended for home consumption must be labelled and packed in this compartment under official supervision, the labels being supplied by the Revenue officers after the duty has been paid. The spirits and sugar used for flavouring or sweetening must be stored in an approved and secure compartment, and used and accounted for in the presence of an official.

The process of manufacture follows very much the

lines on which it is carried on in an Excise factory. The tobacco is usually received in hogsheads, and these are weighed on receipt. The leaf is steamed that it may open easily ; if unstemmed it undergoes the stripping process or removal of the midrib ; if stemmed, this stripping is of course unnecessary. The tobacco is next wetted down, and it is here that the sugar or sweetening matter is added. The leaf if intended for cut or cigarette tobacco is next cut with a knife by machinery, and subsequently more or less " stoved " or heated over a hot plate. If intended for capstan or navy cut it is pressed into flat cakes by means of hydraulic presses. These cakes are subsequently flaked by a knife machine. The real Cavendish or Negrohead (the latter so called from its blackness) is made from Virginia leaf which has been treated by steaming or sweating in order to darken it. It is then placed in long moulds something like gridirons in appearance, and pressed into cakes or bars. The Cavendish is flat, while the Negrohead is twisted. The darker kinds are cooked in hot presses to produce colour and flavour.

All these various processes take place under the supervision of the Revenue officials. Various accounts are kept both by the trader and the officers. When Cavendish is intended for home consumption the required amount on which duty has been paid is weighed out, removed to the duty compartment, and labelled in the officer's presence. The labels must be so wrapped round each packet, that the packet cannot be opened without destroying the wrapper. When labelled the packets must be sent out from the factory forthwith. These precautions are necessary to prevent fraud on the Revenue.

For exportation, the trader may pack the tobacco as he thinks fit, but always under Revenue supervision.

If made up into packets, a fair number of the empty packets or boxes are weighed and duly averaged. The cases are also tared and from these data the officer subsequently obtains the net weight of the tobacco in each case after he has taken the gross weight of the packed case or cases. The cases are then sealed with the Crown seal. Cigarettes, and cigars are tared and averaged in a similar manner, viz., so many cigarettes to the ounce, and so many cigars to the pound. Cases for exportation are all marked with a progressive number, and also their gross and net weights.

By the Finance Act of 1915 manufacturers of Cavendish and Negrohead tobacco are paid an allowance of twopence per pound for every pound of home-grown tobacco employed in making such tobacco.

Waste, refuse, and stalks from a bonded factory may be destroyed or removed to a nicotine factory, or exported as offal snuff. Reference has been made to the various accounts kept, and by means of these a complete record of the traders' operations and stock are obtained. An annual stocktaking is carried out by the Revenue officials, and a reasonable allowance is made for waste in the course of manufacture. Samples are taken in the duty compartment to see that the trader keeps within the moisture limit, but, as a matter of fact, the moisture is low, and averages little over 20 per cent. It will be seen from all the precautions taken, there is little likelihood of any leakage of Revenue in a bonded tobacco factory.

CHAPTER XI

SNUFF

A FRIAR named Romano Pane, who went with Christopher Columbus on one of his voyages to America, was responsible for the introduction of tobacco into Europe. He observed that the Indians snuffed tobacco, reduced to powder, through a long cane. He brought tobacco to Europe, and it was first used in the form of snuff by kings and princes. Its medicinal properties were greatly admired and largely advertised, and thus snuff-taking became so popular on the Continent that its use in churches was prohibited.

In early days each snuff-taker manufactured his own snuff. He carried a round box, containing a *carotte*, or small roll of tobacco, a kind of nutmeg-grater, and a small shovel. With these implements he made his own snuff, and took it when required. Snuff so made was called *tabac rapé*, hence the name rappee applied nowadays to black snuff.

The practice of snuff-taking spread from the Continent to these islands. Tobacco was smoked in England, but taken as snuff in Scotland and Ireland. The practice ultimately spread to England, and in the early part of the eighteenth century it had become the fashion. Ladies took snuff, and gentlemen of the period carried most elegant snuff-boxes. In the time of George IV, snuff had become a most expensive luxury, and it was served up according to the time of day.

At this period it became a mixed commodity. The powdered tobacco was coloured and then perfumed by the admixture of various scents. It is curious to note that, amongst the snuffs of that day were such varieties as Scotch, Taddy's and Prince's Mixture, varieties which remain to the present day. Another variety discovered by accident, was known as Lundy Foot. This was the result of a Dublin fire, the tobacco accidentally burned being subsequently sold and taken as snuff.

Snuffs of to-day are of two kinds, i.e. dry or moist, Moist snuffs are made from leaves, stalks and smalls, while dry snuffs are manufactured principally from stalks of tobacco. Of moist varieties we have Prince's Mixture, and Rappee, and of dry snuffs we have Scotch and high-dried. Wilson's S.P. is, perhaps, the most famous snuff of to-day in the dry class, and Prince's Mixture in the wet class.

In the manufacture of moist snuffs of the Rappee variety the stalks, leaves, etc., are placed in a heap in a square wooden bin. Water is added, together with a salt solution, the limits of the latter being strictly fixed by law, and the whole mass is left to ferment for several weeks. A long thermometer with a wooden handle is thrust into the centre of the mass, and the rising temperature is continuously noted as fermentation progresses. It is curious to smell the pungent odour of a snuff " cure," as it is called ; the strong ammoniacal smell prevailing as the cure proceeds brings tears to the eyes. The mass is turned occasionally to prevent its becoming charred, and the temperature, usually starting about 90° F., must not be allowed to rise above 130° F. The " cure " is removed at the end of three to six weeks, according to the rate of fermentation and subsequently ground in a mill, and finally perfumed.

In manufacturing Welsh, Scotch, or Irish snuff, all of which are known as " Dry snuffs," the stalks are wetted either with water or an alkaline solution and fermented in bins. If Welsh snuff is required, the mass is partially

burned or "toasted" in a special furnace. When
Scotch snuff is required the materials are ground without
toasting, immediately after fermentation is completed.
The Scotch varieties are usually scented, but high-dried
varieties such as Irish and Welsh are not scented.

Certain ingredients only are allowed in snuff manufacture. Lime, added as lime water to Welsh or Irish
snuff, must not exceed 1 per cent. The total of lime and
magnesia must not exceed 13 per cent. The total
alkaline salts (i.e. salts which in solution, turn red
litmus paper blue) and in which the carbonates, chlorides,
and sulphates of Potassium and Sodium, and the
Carbonate of Ammonium are included, must not exceed
26 per cent.

In addition, certain oils are allowed for scenting
purposes. These essential oils consist of such spices, etc.,
as cinnamon and cassia, cloves, otto of roses, lavender,
bergamot, oil of bitter almonds, and other scented
barks and extracts dissolved in spirits. These essential
oils are added to snuffs according to variety and flavour,
and their proportion is usually a trade secret known
only to the manufacturer. ·Tonquin beans are also
allowed for scenting purposes in snuff.

It should be mentioned that there is much waste in
tobacco manufacture. This waste, consisting of stalks,
shorts, smalls, and other refuse such as returns, is
deposited by the manufacturer in the King's warehouse,
and the duty (called drawback) repaid thereon according
to the standard fixed as regards organic and mineral
matter. This waste is known as offal, and when ground
for deposit is termed offal snuff. This snuff is used for
making sheepwash, horticultural fumigant, etc., according to certain prescribed regulations. All snuff exported
or deposited in the King's warehouse, and on which
drawback is claimed, is sampled by the Customs officials

and analytically examined in the Government Laboratory. The payment of drawback follows the certificate of analysis, according to the standard above mentioned.

In bygone days snuff was largely adulterated. Dye, wood, starch, valonia, bog-moss, and other adulterants were introduced according to the variety of snuff. A rigid enforcement of the tobacco laws has gradually stamped out these forms of adulterations, and the snuffs of to-day are pure and wholesome.

The principal reason for the decrease in popularity of the eighteenth-century snuff-box has been the competition of the cigarette. To-day, however, an increasing number of people are finding in snuff an excellent antidote to colds and influenza, and perhaps the day is not far distant when the trade will receive a welcome stimulus from doctors' prescriptions ordering their patients to "sniff to be healthy." Certainly in recent years there has been a growing trade in medicated snuffs; and in 1935-6 a number of manufacturing firms reported double and treble sales of snuff compared with only a year or two before that date. Imports support the view that snuff is returning to favour, for in 1932-3 they were nil, and in 1933-4 5 lb. were imported, but in 1934-5 the imports had risen to 38 lb. Because of the universal popularity of the cigarette, snuff certainly will never regain its former position, but it will occupy a much more important place in the dealer's sales than during the first quarter of the twentieth century.

TOBACCO IN THE LABORATORY

The work done by the Government Chemist in connection with the examination of tobacco for Revenue purposes in the past year was as follows—

Imported and Home Grown Tobacco. The number of samples of imported unmanufactured tobacco received from bonded warehouses for determination of the percentage of moisture was 181.

Twelve samples of imported leaf tobacco were found to contain substances not permitted to be present in tobacco and were therefore held to be inadmissible.

Four hundred and thirty samples of imported manufactured tobacco, cigarettes, and snuff were submitted for classification as to the proper tariff description and rate of duty chargeable if found to be admissible. Three hundred and thirty of these, including 326 samples of cigarettes, were found to contain ingredients which are not allowed to be used in tobacco in this country and which, therefore, rendered the consignments inadmissible for importation. Three samples of imported material resulting from tobacco manufacturing operations were ruled to be inadmissible as "snuff work." In the case of nine samples entered as free of duty, and described as medicinal preparations, the examination showed that no tobacco was present.

Of home grown leaf tobacco, which is being cultivated in East Anglia and the South of England, nine samples were examined.

Manufactured Tobacco for Home Consumption. To ensure the obs rvance of the regulations as to moisture and oil, samples are taken from the finished roll and cut tobacco in the factories and on the premises of retail dealers, as a check on the output of the manufacturers. The percentage of moisture was determined in 6,973 samples and the percentage of oil in 516 samples taken by Customs and Excise officers in this connection. Three samples of oil used under these regulations were examined with a view to approval.

Manufactured Tobacco and Commercial Snuff for Exportation on Drawback. The number of samples involved in claims for drawback on exportation of manufactured tobacco, including cigarettes, cigars, and snuff, was 99,595. Of these 418 samples were commercial snuffs.

Offal Tobacco, Shorts, Smalls, and Stalks of Tobacco deposited on Drawback for Denaturing, Abandonment, the Manufacture of Nicotine or Sheep Dips, or for Exportation. The samples examined under this head were 55,850. Of these 38,500 were stalks and 17,350 offal snuff, shorts, and smalls.

Miscellaneous. One hundred and four samples of unmanufactured and manufactured tobacco, and 15 samples of original leaf were taken from Bonded Tobacco Factories for control purposes.

Ninety-one samples of nicotine preparations and insecticides were examined; of these 59 were from imported goods. The object of this examination was to ascertain whether the articles were sufficiently free from constituents of tobacco, other than nicotine, to allow of importation or delivery, free of duty, from bonded warehouses. With the exception of one sample, found to possess the character of tobacco extract, all were approved.

One hundred and four samples of essences and essential oils were submitted for approval for use in flavouring tobacco, and 29 samples of materials were examined for ascertaining if they could be used as adhesive for the paper wrappers of cigarettes.

CHAPTER XII

IMPORTS

FOR many years the tobacco trade of the United Kingdom had all its eggs in one basket. That basket belonged to Uncle Sam. The position is illustrated by the fact that in 1911 we took 104,329,000 lb. of tobacco from the United States in comparison with only 14,541,000 lb. from all other sources. This preeminence has been enjoyed by the United States ever since the discovery of tobacco in the sixteenth century. American leaf is the staple leaf but, as will be shown later in this work, our dependence on this source of supply will probably not be so marked in years to come by reason of the development of the tobacco-growing industry within the Briti h Empire. American unmanufactured tobacco consists of Virginian and Western leaf, the former being grown near the eastern coast and the latter farther inland There are dark and bright Virginia leaf grown in Virginia and the Carolinas, used for cigarettes and for making light coloured mixtures. The bulk of the tobacco grown for pipe smoking comes from the region known as the old belt, Kentucky, Tennessee, and is known as Western leaf.

British cigar manufacturers get seed leaf from the United States, the seed being sent annually from Cuba. Leaf used for making British cigars (which on account of high taxation is now a dwindling industry) consists of Sumatra, Borneo, and Havana. Some quantities also come from South America. What are known as " substitute " tobaccos, that is, tobaccos used for

BOX-MAKING AND LABELLING

BOXING TWEENIES

By permission of

Messrs. Martin, Ltd.

blending with American leaf, come from Java, Japan, China and other places.

The Turkish cigarette manufacturer imports leaf from Asiatic Turkey and from the territory known as Turkey in Europe. Some is transhipped from Egypt, but little or no tobacco is grown in that country. Much of the leaf grown in Java and other tropical regions is sent to Bremen and Amsterdam, which are tobacco depots, and this accounts for the large quantities of tobacco coming to this country from Germany and the Netherlands.

Until thirty years ago, putting the American War of Secession aside, British manufacturers had little difficulty in procuring all the leaf they needed from American planters at reasonable prices, but the formation of " pools " by the planters led to trouble. Prices were raised by the regulation of supplies. The Imperial Tobacco Company, Ltd., thereupon set about finding alternative sources of supply. Hence the birth of the Empire tobacco-growing industry. For the first time in 350 years' history of the tobacco trade a British Colony—Nyasaland—began to supply the English market with good tobacco leaf. In four years the quantity rose from 175,000 lb. to 1,361,000 lb.

The success of the industry in Nyasaland led to other Colonies and Dominions taking it up, and since the introduction of the preference tariff it has shown an increasing prosperity. Some idea of the extent to which the industry has expanded within the confines of the British Empire is evident from the fact that to-day tobacco is being grown in Northern and Southern Rhodesia, Nyasaland, Canada, Australia, India, New Zealand, British North Borneo, Burma, Ceylon, Cyprus, Jamaica, Kenya, Leeward Isles, Mauritius, Montserrat, Palestine, Union of South Africa, Tanganyika Territory, Trinidad, and

Uganda. Not in all these cases is there an exportable surplus as yet, but there is little doubt that in due time each of these places will send tobacco to the United Kingdom, the only · real danger being that of over-production at the expense of quality.

Each year has seen a steady increase in the quantity of Empire manufactured tobacco consumed in this country, and the next few years will see a great expansion of the area of land within the Empire under cultivation for the production of tobacco. In Rhodesia alone in 1936 it was estimated there were 2,000,000 acres of fine tobacco land waiting to be cultivated, while in Uganda large tracts of land have been found to be suitable and await development.

The consumption of Empire tobacco in the United Kingdom in 1935–6 was 45,107,735 lb., and considerably over half of this total came from the Rhodesias and Nyasaland. Research work is taking place in nearly all of the tobacco-growing districts of the Empire, and the knowledge gained in this direction can only lead to the production of a leaf more palatable to the English smoker, the market to which the Colonial grower naturally looks for the sale of his product. That Empire tobaccos can more than hold their own with the American types is evident from the fact that not only has the English pipe smoker taken kindly to it, but on 1st May, 1936, there appeared in *Tobacco* (Industrial Newspapers, Ltd.) the statement: "The pipe trade is already almost entirely Empire."

The rate of duty on unmanufactured tobacco, stripped or stemmed, 10 lb. or more moisture in every 100 lb., is 9s. 6d. per lb., but as from 11th September, 1931, there has been a preference of 2s. 0½d. per lb. on tobacco "consigned from and grown, produced or manufactured within the British Empire," and in his Budget statement on 26th April, 1926, the Chancellor of the Exchequer said the Government would guarantee preference for a period of ten years. In the financial year 1935–6, the latest year for which statistics are available, we imported 122,913,943 lb. of unmanufactured tobacco at the full rate of duty and 45,107,735 lb. at the preferential rate. In that year, therefore, the proportion of Empire tobacco to foreign-grown was 37 per cent, the highest figure yet reached. Of the total imports of Empire tobacco, 15,077,128 lb. came from the Rhodesias, and 10,109,996 lb. from Nyasaland, these two parts of the Empire supplying 55·8 per cent of all tobacco imported under preference duties. It is interesting to note that between the years 1932–3 and 1935–6 the imports of Empire tobacco increased from 32,499,059 lb. to 45,107,735 lb., an increase of 12,608,676 lb. in three years, its proportion to foreign grown imports increasing in the same period from 27·5 to 37 per cent. In the same period of three years imports at the full rate of duty only increased by 4,886,486 lb.

At home experiments have been made in recent years to grow tobacco on a commercial scale. At Church Crookham, in Hampshire, these experiments have been brought to a successful issue, thanks to Government help and English-grown manufactured tobacco and cigarettes are now obtainable at a number of shops. The crop could be increased very easily should the demand grow, and the cultivation and handling of this tobacco would provide considerable employment. In the year 1935–6 the quantity of English-grown tobacco produced was 3,476 lb.

No reference to the Empire tobacco industry would be complete without mention of recent events in Ireland.

In Dublin and in certain other towns in the south of

MAKING TWEENIES

CIGAR MAKING (BOYS)

By permission of

Messrs. Martin, Ltd.

Ireland the manufacture of tobacco was for many years
a flourishing industry. Irish manufacturers had not
only a good inland trade, but they shipped considerable
quantities of tobacco and cigarettes to Great Britain
besides having a large export trade to the colonies
and to many foreign countries. The political troubles
which overwhelmed that unhappy country had their
effect upon the industry, and one of the first acts of the
Government of the Irish Free State, after the granting
of Home Rule, was to place a stinging import tax on
manufactured tobacco. The effect was immediate.
Irish manufacturers reaped a rich harvest at the expense
of their English competitors, but it was not for long.
Some branches of the Imperial Tobacco Company, such
as W. D. & H. O. Wills, of Bristol, either purchased or
erected factories within the Free State in order to retain
their Irish trade. The net result has been to provide
employment for a greater number of persons within the
Free State, but a considerable proportion of these extra
workers were sent across from England.

For many years experiments have been made in
growing tobacco in Ireland. The Imperial Government
gave assistance by way of subsidy, but the growers
found the new Free State Government much less sym-
pathetic. Under considerable pressure the Minister of
Finance, early in 1926, appointed a Commission to
inquire into and report on the prospects before the
industry, at the same time indicating his own view
that the State could not render help. The Commission
took evidence from the growers and from manufacturers,
both of whom testified that something might be done
to build up the industry if financial help could be given.
A Government witness took the line that the growing
of tobacco on a commercial scale was foredoomed to
failure. The Commission, at the end of March, recom-

mended State assistance, but the Minister of Finance rejected the proposal out of hand without consulting his colleagues. Such, at all events, was the report current at the time.

Since that date the opinion of the Government has altered considerably to the benefit of the tobacco grower, whose output each year is increasing. In 1935 about 500,000 lb., or 6 per cent of the country's requirements, were grown in the Irish Free State, compared with 68,000 lb. in 1909. Home-grown tobacco received a welcome stimulus as the result of an Order issued by the Executive Council of the Irish Free State in 1936 making it obligatory on Irish manufacturers to mix the home-grown leaf with imported tobacco, the home leaf being divided on a quota basis, having regard to the class of tobacco produced by each manufacturer during the preceding twelve months.

Manufactured tobacco imported into the United Kingdom represents only a small proportion of the quantity of tobacco actually going into consumption. This section of the trade consists mainly of Cuban cigars and American Cavendish and Negrohead, with some cigarettes and pipe tobaccos. The consumption figures for the three years 1932–5 are given in the following table—

	Quantities—lb.			Net Receipts—£.		
	1932–3	1933–4	1934–5	1932–3	1933–4	1934–5
Cigars	254,773	344,292	418,907	223,103	303,465	370,928
Cigarettes	64,525	65,272	59,529	46,934	47,534	43,268
Cavendish	57,540	49,349	48,156	39,413	33,777	32,958
Snuff	—	5	38	—	2	23
Other Sorts	10,484	9,500	9,272	5,419	4,892	4,788
Totals	387,322	468,418	535,902	314,869	389,670	451,965

The snuff mentioned above is " offal " snuff, used for

nicotine extract and other insecticide purposes. It will be seen how great is the discrepancy between the total imports of unmanufactured tobacco, in 1935–6—168,021,678 lb.—and those of manufactured—735,705 lb.

EXPORTS
BRITISH MANUFACTURED TOBACCOS

Fiscal influences have left deep fissures in the tobacco trade and one of these cracks is visibly shown in the export branch. There are two classes of exporters of British manufactured tobaccos—the shipper from the bonded factories, and the shipper from the " licensed " factories. A bonded factory is a warehouse the proprietor of which has to enter into a bond for the safeguarding of the revenue. As will be seen in the figures stated below, the bulk of the export trade falls to the owners of the licensed factories.

	lb.
Exports of manufactured tobacco of all kinds, excluding stalks etc., and snuff, made in bond for year 1932–3..	997,419
Exports of manufactured tobacco of all kinds, excluding stalks etc., and snuff, made in the licensed factories for year 1932–3	16,512,489
Total .. .. .·.	17,509,908

What is the difference between these two classes of manufacturers ?   It is this : one works on duty-free leaf, the other on duty-paid leaf. Thus in one case there is no capital locked up in the form of duty payment whilst in the other case capital is locked up.   On exportation the bonded manufacturer is free from any trouble connected with the return of the duty whilst the " licensed " factory man has to go through certain

TOBACCO FOR TWEENIES

By permission of   WRAPPER TOBACCO WAREHOUSE   Messrs. Martin, Ltd.

formalities in order to get back the duty formerly paid on the leaf used in making the exported article. It is always a nice question for experts to adjudge the exact amount of leaf and duty paid thereon which the manufactured article represents. Should the equivalent returned by the Customs to the exporter be actually less than the sum originally paid, then it naturally follows that the goods are saddled with an extra cost from which the bonded competitor is free. On the other hand, should the Customs return more than the equivalent, then such extra money represents so much subsidy. Whether the sum be too little or too much there would be inequality established with a consequent undue preference to one side or the other. Hence the paramount importance of determining a full and fair sum, so as to hold the scales of justice evenly in the interests of both classes of exporters. The sum returned is technically known as " drawback." Until 1904 the exporter on drawback was greatly handicapped, inasmuch as he did not get returned to him the sums he was fairly entitled to receive. With loss formerly facing the manufacturers and the need for building up a big export trade, recourse was had to the acquisition of and manufacture in bonded factories—a costly undertaking—where the manufacture was under the daily supervision and control of the Customs officials. These particular bonded factories were established by Mr. Gladstone in 1863, not so much for the purpose of an export trade as for supplying the home trade with sweetened tobacco called " Cavendish and Negrohead." Any surplus left over after supplying the needs of the home trade was allowed to be exported.

Like Topsy of old, Mr. Gladstone's " surplus " has " growed." It follows from this that the product of these bonded Cavendish factories is a sweetened or

flavoured article in order to conform with the requirements of Mr. Gladstone's Manufactured Tobacco Act
of 1863. Now the licensed manufacturer is not permitted by law to make any sweetened tobacco in his
" licensed " factory. Hence, legally speaking, whilst
one manufacturer exports a sweetened tobacco, the
other exports an unsweetened tobacco. For reasons
which need not be mentioned here this difference is
more apparent than real. Out of a total export in 1932–3
of 997,419 lb. from these bonded factories, only 9,438 lb.
consisted of cigarettes. In 1904 a Customs and Excise
Departmental Committee of Experts was appointed by
the Treasury to draw up full and fair drawback rates for
the "licensed" factory exporter with a view to recouping
him for the outlay rendered necessary by his payment of
the duty. The idea was to place him in the same position
as if no duty had existed, and in this way he would be
enabled to stand more or less on an equality, in foreign
and colonial markets, with his big bonded competitor.
This was done to the satisfaction of the manufacturers
concerned. Different rates of drawback were established
for different classes of tobacco. The present "Full"
duty on leaf tobacco is 9s. 6d. per lb. Taking into consideration Customs requirements, losses and waste in
manufacture, and loss of interest on capital, the Tobacco
Drawback Committee found that the drawback on cigars
should be at the rate of 9s. 1d. per lb., cigarettes 8s. 10d.
per lb., cut and roll tobaccos 8s. 10d. per lb., snuff 8s. 7d.
per lb.

The "Full" drawback rates have since been increased
to—cigars 10s. 9d. lb.; cigarettes 10s. 6d. lb.; cut and
roll tobaccos 10s. 3d. lb.; and snuff 10s. lb.

It is only by the establishment of proper rates of
drawback that an export trade by the licensed manufacturer becomes possible. Since the institution of such

the export trade has largely passed from the bonded factory to the "licensed" factory. It must be remembered that if care be not exercised in granting drawback a great loss of revenue will accrue. There has been much money lost in the past to the Crown through the drawback door, by misrepresentation and fraud, especially in the tobacco trade. A watchful eye is ever necessary, and the difficulty is to steer such a between course as to facilitate the path of the exporter on the one hand and at the same time to safeguard the revenue on the other.

Tobacco is an article that all civilized nations tax. In most cases this tax is an import duty. Some countries, like France, forbid importation in the interests of the Régie. In other countries, like the United States, the import duty is high in the interest of home manufactures. Fluctuation of these rates of duty is always a factor for British tobacco exporters to contend with, and these changes affect more or less the volume of the British export trade.

The principal overseas customers of the British manufacturer are China, British India, Straits Settlements, and New Zealand.

One word as to the export British cigar trade.

The cigar is the aristocrat of the smoking world, and generally gets aristocratic treatment in the form of the highest tariff rate. Hence its entry into foreign and colonial markets is handicapped by its additional duty price. Another factor that militates against British cigar exporters is that the cigar, being a hand labour product, creates prejudice against its importation as a displacer of labour. Although great art is required in properly making a cigar, yet the rough rolling up of leaves into cigars can readily be performed abroad, and such home-made products lessen the demand for British imported cigars.   These are some of the reasons to account for the small export trade of the British cigar.

EXPORT OF BRITISH PRODUCED " OFFALS "

The term " offal " includes the waste arising in course of .manufacture· The " shorts " arising from handling leaf, the " smalls " from making cigarettes, the " dust " accumulating from all sources of manufacture, and the "stalks," or midribs, of tobacco leaves—all are comprised within the above title. Some of this offal is made into insecticides, some treated for the nicotine extract, and some exported untreated to the Argentine and other countries for the use of agriculturists, etc.

SHIPS STORES

The Customs Authorities permit duty-free tobacco and other dutiable stores to be taken on board ship for the use of each person on board. In order to prevent abuse of this privilege, and so safeguard the revenue, certain Customs restrictions have to be complied with. To minimize opportunities for re-landing this duty-free tobacco, supplies are limited per voyage per man per day. For outward-bound ships one ounce is the unit. Tobacco for the Navy is ordered through the captain of each of H.M. ships. Troopships and transports get the privilege of receiving duty-free tobacco, also foreign men-of-war. Drawback is paid to the licensed manufacturer supplying direct from his factory. This ships stores trade is important and developing. It is not included under the heading of exports.

PARCELS POST

No statistics are published showing the number of post parcels received into, and dispatched, from the

United Kingdom containing tobacco. The incoming post parcels are examined by a special staff of the Customs stationed at the Post Office. The duty on the tobacco, etc., contained in each parcel, together with a " fine " of 6d. per lb., is assessed by the Customs and collected by the postman on delivery. The total quantity coming in and going out by parcel post is included in the imports and exports.

HOME CONSUMPTION

Home consumption returns are scarred with the frequent ruthless batterings of the fiscal ram. The Free Trade policy is to tax comparatively a few articles, especially those of national indulgence, solely for revenue purposes. The main result of this policy is the raising of an enormous revenue from articles like beer, spirits, and tobacco. Unfortunately the need to raise more money has compelled finance ministers, again and again, to lay siege to these few revenue producers. The result of these continual assaults has been bad to the trade and to the consumer. Traders develop nerves and sustain upset and loss. They live and work more or less in suspense, and as increased duties mean more working capital, the higher the duty the more difficult becomes the path of the smaller manufacturers. The tobacco consumer is irritated by a continued upward price of his brand and either smokes less or selects a cheaper kind. Recovery follows after a year or two, and progress continues till the next " visitation," when the vicious cycle is again repeated.

The consumption of tobacco in the financial year 1935–6 was 168,757,383 lb., on which the State received revenue amounting to £74,993,036.

Features of the home trade in recent years have been the enormous increase in the use of cigarettes and pipe tobaccos and the decline in the consumption of cigars. The Havana cigar manufacturers have for some time made strenuous efforts to recover their position in the English market, and with a certain measure of success, for we are still one of Cuba's best customers, but fashions in smoking, as in almost everything else, seem to have changed. The cigarette is everywhere ; the pipe nearly everywhere ; the cigar scarcely anywhere. The decline in the popularity of the cigar can hardly be attributed wholly to increased taxation, for taxation on other forms of tobacco is heavy too. The truth is more likely to lie in the fact that the smoking of a cigar is something of a ceremony, the rites of which people have little inclination for in these days of haste and hurry.

CHAPTER XIII

Not every pound weight of duty-paid unmanufactured tobacco is retained for home consumption. Nearly 10 per cent goes back again in the form of waste to the Customs, who return to the manufacturers the duty originally paid upon it. This refuse tobacco consists of the midribs of the leaves, called " stalks," broken pieces, dust, cigarette waste or " smalls," and damaged tobacco—all classed under the general term of " offals." A tobacco leaf in growing is amplexicaul, that is, the base of the leaf clasps the parent stem. This base is narrow, and in the act of binding the curved leaves into " hands " the blade or lamina portion gets rubbed off by the planters, leaving the midrib bare. Hence the general impression that tobacco leaves have petioles or stalks ; but such is not the case. When " bird's-eye " tobacco was more popular than it is to-day, manufacturers were able to cut up the entire leaf, and the cross section with its familiar " horse-shoe " or " bird's-eye " appearance revealed the presence of the woody midrib. Nowadays smokers prefer their tobaccos without this midrib, and as the practice of " snuffing " is no longer popular, the manufacturer is unable to utilize his " stalks." In the United States tobacco stalks constitute so much litter but in the United Kingdom the dutiable value alone is 9s. 6d. per lb. (Full Rate). Revenue exigencies have compelled the Treasury to take back all this tobacco waste and return the duty thereon. It then becomes duty-free, and the care of the Customs lies in preventing this duty-free stuff getting back again into the hands of the manufacturers. It is either destroyed or exported. On account of their germicidal properties, tobacco extracts and powders are greatly sought after by agriculturists, and in order to meet this demand the Customs permit manufacturers to make these substances in specially approved bonded warehouses under the supervision and control of revenue officials.   Thus the valuable alkaloid nicotine is prepared, and various ingredients added to the " offals" for making insecticides both in the liquid and dry form.   Great revenue care is taken in prescribing the ingredients, which cannot be easily separated afterwards from the tobacco.   Their presence can be readily detected at the Government Laboratory in the event of any illegal attempt to present the denatured duty-free " offals " once more for the drawback allowance.   Past experience has taught the revenue custodians the pressing need for skilled chemists to stand at the drawback gate.   In making nicotine, etc., any refuse left is burnt in the presence of a Customs officer.   Hop powder contains sulphur, asafoetida, and sago flour. Sheep wash has common salt, blue vitriol, and oil of turpentine.   Fumigants contain hellebore, saltpetre, asafoetida, cayenne, lampblack, and sago flour.   Tobacco extract contains soft soap.   All the ingredients require to be examined by the official chemists before being used ; likewise all the tobacco insecticides when manufactured.   A lot of the tobacco manufacturer's " offals " are not rich enough in nicotine properties and so are left on the hands of the Customs, who have them burnt, bags and all, in the parish dust destructor, an officer witnessing the destruction. Suitable stalks are imported duty-free for ¦the insecticide factories, and agriculturists are now desiring to grow tobacco plants specially for the production of cheaper nicotine. ˙Naturally the Chancellor of the Exchequer and his staff think of the revenue drawback door and look askance at such a proposal.

CHAPTER XIV

SMUGGLING

THAT romantic tribe of swashbucklers and smugglers, the Dick Hatterick fraternity, has long gone the way of snuff boxes and adulterators. High duties undoubtedly favour smuggling, but whether high or low it is very doubtful whether smuggling ever will die out. The nearest approach to the Dick Hatterick of former days is the ubiquitous Dutch cooper, who supplies British and Irish fishermen on board their smacks with cheap grog and baccy. Sometimes the bold Dutchman ventures within the three-mile limit and gets pounced upon by the patrolling British navy. Smuggling nowadays principally takes the form of secretion of small quantities by persons coming either from the Continent or board ship, especially at naval ports.

The latter case is an abuse of the ships stores privilege of receiving duty-free tobacco, etc. All vessels coming from the Continent are closely rummaged by Customs experts, and now and then " finds " result to the discomfiture of the venturesome smuggler. Fishermen and other persons may successfully run the gauntlet of naval and Customs supervision, and land their tobacco and cigars, but only to meet with confiscation on shore. A lower selling price with underselling attracts the attention of competitors and leads to complaints. There are too many people about nowadays for the smuggler's purpose.

In olden times the few families living in remote hamlets were confederates, but the growth of population destroyed the secrecy of a " run." What other causes have led to the decline of smuggling ? Patrolling ships and coastguards, scientific discovery with its improved means of communication and detection, better revenue administration, fewer and scattered factories, entailing greater responsibility and risk in receiving raw tobacco, and lastly, the increased number of retail shop-keepers, causing keener competition and greater risk of publicity to the smuggling of manufactured tobaccos. Supplies of confiscated tobacco in sound condition were sent, as is now usual, to Criminal Lunatic Asylums and to State Inebriate Reformatories. The tobacco unfit for human consumption, but useful for fumigating purposes, was sent to the Botanic Gardens at Kew and Edinburgh. This is putting the tobacco to a better use than con-signing it to the historic " King's Pipe."

CHAPTER XV

TARIFF AND LICENCE DUTIES

THE following is the tobacco tariff of the United Kingdom :—

	Full Rate per lb.		Preferential Rate per lb.	
TOBACCO—	*s.*	*d.*	*s.*	*d.*
Unmanufactured, unstripped or unstemmed—				
Containing 10 lb. or more of moisture in every 100 lb. weight thereof	9	6	7	5½
Containing less than 10 lb. of moisture in every 100 lb. weight thereof	10	6	8	2⅞
Unmanufactured, stripped or stemmed—				
Containing 10 lb. or more of moisture in every 100 lb. weight thereof	9	6½	7	5⅞
Containing less than 10 lb. of moisture in every 100 lb. weight thereof	10	6½	8	3¼
Cigars	18	1	14	2¼
Cigarettes	14	7	11	5¼
Cavendish and Negrohead	13	9	10	9⅜
Cavendish and Negrohead manufactured in Bond	12	–	9	4⅞
Other manufactured tobacco	12	–	9	4⅞
Snuff containing more than 13 lb. of moisture in every 100 lb. weight thereof	11	4	8	10⅝
Snuff not containing more than 13 lb. of moisture in every 100 lb. weight thereof	13	9	10	9⅜

The important part that moisture plays in the duty on unmanufactured tobacco will not escape notice. Manufacturers are alive to this factor and take the precaution to dry their leaf and strips abroad before importing them into the United Kingdom. Some manufacturers, especially the smaller men, are compelled to use a wetter leaf than that used by their wealthier competitors, and so are compelled to pay duty on more moisture and proportionately less tobacco. A demand has arisen to remedy this state of affairs by basing the duty so that the excess water in tobacco shall be allowed for.

There is a great difference between the duty on the raw article and the duty on the imported manufactured article. Were the tariff to be revised on a strictly Free Trade basis the present rates on imported cigars, etc., could not be justified. Originally, in 1863, this tariff was so based by Mr. Gladstone, but his data were inaccurate and incomplete. Since then the rise of the cigarette industry and the superiority of the imported article led finance ministers to impose discriminating and higher rates on cigarettes and cigars.

The tariff history of tobacco is one long record of change. Formerly there were Customs duties and Excise duties, British duties and Irish duties, preferential duties to the American colony and protectionist duties to the foreigner. Every few years from 1769 onwards saw changes in the tariff and always in an upward direction. The peaceful days to the trade were the two middle quarters of the nineteenth century with a 3s. duty and 5 per cent, but even then the number of manufacturers continued to decrease. In fact this decrease has been in operation for the last hundred years, but the rate of decline has been more rapid during the last ten years than it was in the preceding fifty years.

Tobacco manufacturers are required to pay licence duty according to the quantity of raw tobacco received into their factories. The scale is shown on page 108.

The pro rata licence duty stops at the 100,000 lb. limit, thereby falling proportionately lighter on the manufacturer outside this limit and heavier on the manufacturer inside.

Wholesale dealers pay 5s. 3d. per year, the same as a

TOBACCO

TOBACCO AND SNUFF MANUFACTURERS

		£	s.	d
If the unmanufactured tobacco received in the preceding year ending 5th July does not exceed 20,000 lb.	=	5	5	0

lb.

			£	s.	d
Exceeds 20,000 lb. and does not exceed	40,000	=	10	10	0
Exceeds 40,000 lb. and does not exceed	60,000	=	15	15	0
Exceeds 60,000 lb. and does not exceed	80,000	=	21	0	0
Exceeds 80,000 lb. and does not exceed	100,000	=	26	5	0
Exceeds 100,000 lb.		=	31	10	0
Beginners		=	5	5	0

A surcharge is made on a beginner if he exceeds the 20,000 lb. limit.

retail tobacconist. In days gone by Irish wholesale dealers paid ten guineas per year.

An occasional licence to tobacco dealers costs 4d. per day.

Tobacco growers and curers pay a 5s. licence per annum. The Excise rates for them are as follows :—

Cavendish or Negrohead manufactured in bond .. ..9s. 4⅞d. per lb.

Unmanufactured, containing 10 lb. or more of moisture in every 100 lb. weight thereof .. ..7s. 3½d. per lb.

If containing less than 10 lb. of moisture .. .. 8s. 0⅞d. per lb.

The rate on raw tobacco is 2d. per lb. less than the Customs tariff. This is not a preferential rate. The Excise restrictions are computed to cost the home grower 2d. per lb.

The tobacco tariff in the Isle of Man is the same as the Customs duties of the United Kingdom. The Channel Islands have their own tariff.

APPENDIX

FIRE HAZARDS OF TOBACCO MANUFACTURE

By R. E. Taylor, F.C.I.I.

The purpose of this appendix is to supplement the information contained in this work by supplying some particulars of the fire hazards arising out of the manufacture of tobacco in Great Britain and Ireland. No notice is taken of the curing operations which take place before the tobacco leaf reaches this country, the following notes dealing solely with the risks of storage and manufacture from the time the tobacco enters the bonded warehouse as " unmanufactured tobacco " until it leaves the factory in the form of manufactured goods, ready for distribution.

Warehouses. Tobacco leaf, after arrival on this side, is in the first instance deposited as a rule in bonded warehouses. These warehouses are generally constructed very substantially and in such a manner as to resist the spread of fire, with good fire appliances on the spot or in the neighbourhood. Further, no hazardous processes are carried on in the buildings, consequently the risk of fire is not a serious one.

On the other hand, it must be borne in mind that a very disastrous fire occurred as recently as 14th April, 1923, in a tobacco warehouse at Victoria Dock, London, the total loss being about £1,150,000. The fire broke out about 2.30 a.m. while the warehouse was locked up, and the cause is unknown.

Tobacco is very susceptible to damage by smoke and by the water used in extinguishing a fire. Some classes of merchandise, when a fire obtains a hold, feed the flames to such an extent that the goods speedily vanish into air, leaving not a rack behind, while some other commodities burn less rapidly, but are destroyed quite as effectively by water and smoke.

Flimsy drapery goods fall under the former category and tobacco under the latter. In both cases the result, from the fire underwriter's point of view, is the same, namely, a total loss. It is therefore advisable, when estimating the chances of loss in a tobacco warehouse, to take into account not only the risk of a fire breaking out in the warehouse itself, but also the risk of an outbreak in a building in close proximity, through which very serious damage to the stock of tobacco, by water and smoke, might result. It should also be noted that the pungent smoke from a tobacco fire seriously retards the firemen in extinguishing the outbreak.

My Lady Nicotine, if American-born, as is likely, takes the form of a huge wooden barrel or hogshead weighing 1,000 lb. or thereby, so that, undoubtedly, she is a lady of weight as well as of importance. She remains in seclusion in the warehouse for a considerable time, and in due time her owner arranges to pay the Government approximately £450, in order to secure her release. He then arranges for her conveyance to the factory.

Factory Management. In a tobacco factory one or more of the following classes of goods are manufactured, namely, (a) tobacco for smoking and chewing, (b) cigars, (c) cigarettes, and (d) snuff. The number of employees may range from less than 100 in the smaller factories to several thousands in the larger risks.

The larger and more modern factories are models of order and cleanliness, and it is very important that a tobacco factory should be run on these lines. Should there be any laxity in the management, with resultant untidiness, fires may occur in various ways. For example :

tobacco stalks or other refuse (known as " offals ") may be dried in an unauthorized place, such as a boiler house, or the stalks may be placed in a heap on the top of steam pipes, and an outbreak of fire under such conditions is ·not an improbable event.

The canvas cloths and papers used in the manufacture of black rolls may be allowed to accumulate in some corner, and, as these are saturated with olive oil, spontaneous ignition may arise.

The departments where packing or cigarette making is carried on may, if carelessness prevails, soon be littered with loose paper or cardboard, and so form an easy prey to a dropped light.

As regards oily rags and waste—those old enemies of the fire underwriter—the cigarette manufacturer has already declared war upon such refuse, for the excellent reason that it causes serious damage when it comes into contact with his stock ; consequently there is reasonable ground for believing that it will be attacked when discovered and thrown into the boiler fire. With this happy alliance of insured and insurer, the fire waste from this quarter is reduced to a minimum.

The cigarette making and packing machines used in a modern factory have various small appliances attached (heated by gas or electricity) for drying paste or ink, but it is difficult to see how, with ordinary care, any appreciable loss can arise in this connection. Nevertheless, it is on record that a cigarette machine—a wonderful piece of intricate mechanism—was on one occasion very seriously damaged by the heated glass of an electric bulb coming into contact with the cigarette paper.

Drying. Numerous drying operations are carried on in tobacco factories, as mentioned in the textbook, and in most factories the chief physical hazard may be looked for in this direction. It is necessary, therefore, that all heating appliances be carefully examined by the insurance surveyor with a view to ascertaining that they are at a safe distance from all woodwork or other combustible material. In drying stores the temperature may be found to range from 100° F. up to 220° F. or thereby.

All drying stoves should, if practicable, be so constructed and situated as not to jeopardize the main risk, and this is especially necessary in the case of flue-heated stoves. The presence of internal woodwork in stoves should be reduced to a minimum. The public are frequently sceptical when one suggests that a steam pipe in contact with woodwork may cause a fire, but as losses have actually occurred in this way, in a tobacco factory and elsewhere, the insurance surveyor should take up a firm position as to getting such a defect remedied. If the woodwork cannot be removed from the building altogether, arrangements might be made for it to be cut, say, 3 inches clear and the space filled in with uralite, asbestos, or other protective material.

Cigars. Cigars are largely made by hand, and the chief hazard of this department is to be found in the drying room, the temperature of which is about 100° F.

Snuff. Snuff making now form an insignificant portion of the tobacco business, but if such manufacture is carried on. it is advisable that this section of the factory be suitably cut off from the rest of the premises. A set of magnets should be attached to the grinding machinery for the purpose of removing metallic substances which may cause sparking. The presence of tobacco dust adds greatly to the fire hazard of this department, and naked lights should be prohibited, so as to minimize the risk of explosion. The drying arrangements require to be carefully examined.

Incidental Risks. In a large tobacco factory various incidental risks are to be found, and these all add to the fire hazard, especially if, as may happen, the premises are all more or less in communication. It is beyond the scope of these notes to deal at length with the incidental risks referred to, but they are briefly noted below, so that this review of the fire hazards of a tobacco factory may not be incomplete.

The undernoted classes of work may, for example, be done at the tobacco factory instead of in a separate establishment—

Joinery work.
Cardboard box making.
Tin box and canister making.
Printing.

Where work of this kind is done to any appreciable extent, the workshops should form a separate building or buildings.

Further, we must look for the minor hazards found in many up-to-date factories, such as garages for business and private cars and a restaurant for workers.

Common Hazards. Finally, in order to arrive at the sum total of the fire hazards of a tobacco factory, we must include such of the " common hazards " as are applicable. The common hazards which are most likely to be found in a tobacco factory are those arising from exposure, height, floor openings, wood lining and partitions, lighting, heating, ventilation, power, cubical capacity, hazardous goods, spontaneous combustion, and non-removal of waste, subject to the modification in regard to waste in cigarette factories already noted.

The only comment to be made in this connection is that, in regard to the item " hazardous goods," the storage of a moderate quantity of spirits and olive oil may be looked for. If there is a garage, the storage of petrol within the buildings should, of course, be prohibited.

Fire Losses. Mr. O. R. Fabian, in a Paper on " Tobacco Factories," read at the Bristol Insurance Institute in February, 1903 (see Volume VI of the *Journal of the Chartered Insurance Institute*), stated that, so far as his information went, very few fires of any consequence had occurred in tobacco factories. Since then, the fire record of such risks has not been so favourable.

If one desires to arrive at an estimate as to whether the current insurance rates are adequate or otherwise, the experience of the last quarter of a century may be taken as a fair basis of calculation. During that period the records show that, in addition to the warehouse loss of fully £1,000,000 at Victoria Dock, London, already mentioned, there have been quite a number of serious fires on the manufacturing side of the business. For example, a tobacco factory loss of £120,000 heads the list of London fires for the year 1910. This fire, like that at the Victoria Dock warehouse, occurred after the premises had been locked up for the night, the cause being unknown. It is, as a rule, impossible to trace the origin of a fire that is well advanced when the brigade arrives on the scene, and almost all the serious fires during the period under review must be classified, in regard to cause of outbreak, as belonging to the great unknown. On the other hand, in the case of the lesser lights—in other words, the smaller fires—it is not very difficult to ascertain the actual or probable causes, and one must look to them for information as to the chief hazards of a tobacco factory.

The first thing that strikes one in looking over the known or probable causes of fire is that the hazard of the drying operations stands out prominently as the chief sinner, about 50 per cent of the fires being connected with this feature of the business. There is no doubt that if the insurance offices could see their way to frame standard regulations in respect of drying operations and to penalize manufacturers not conforming to such regulations, the fire waste in tobacco factories would be considerably reduced.

As the process of moistening is carried on at the initial stage in all classes of manufacture—tobacco, cigars, cigarettes, and snuff—so also are artificial drying operations to be found at later stages in every description of factory. Drying may not, however, be done in that section of a factory where brown rolls are made, and the manufacture in that department may consist of the innocent processes of moistening, stem stripping, spinning (a little olive oil being used), and making up into rolls.

At least two fires are attributed to spontaneous combustion. Cloths (doubtless saturated with olive oil) in a steam press room were responsible for one of these fires, while another occurred at or about a large heap of tobacco refuse. In the latter case, spontaneous combustion is merely named as a possible cause, and the loss was quite small.

Other known or probable causes of fire, so far as my information goes, are friction of machinery, electric lighting, defective chimney, dropped lights, gas stove, spark from chimney, and hot ashes. It is evident that some of these, as also of those due to drying operations, are really attributable to laxity in management.

Loss **Adjustments.** In estimating the amount of loss likely to arise out of a tobacco fire, one must take into account some special considerations which are peculiar to the trade.

The usual contract of mercantile insurance provides for the merchant receiving payment of the market value of the goods immediately anterior to the fire, but this is not an adequate protection for the tobacco trade. When a serious tobacco fire occurs in a bonded warehouse, on this side, the manufacturer may experience considerable difficulty in replacing his tobacco, and may find that the market price has stiffened after the fire. In order to meet such difficulties, he should effect an insurance providing for the basis of settlement being the original cost plus subsequent charges, interest, appreciation, and extra cost of replacement, not exceeding in all the figure at which the tobacco may be replaced within thirty days after the fire.

Another point is, when should the duty on tobacco—now at a very high rate—be reckoned as part of the fire loss ? The answer to this question is to be found in the attitude of the British Customs Authorities, which may be briefly stated as undernoted—

Tobacco on which duty has not been paid. In the case of accidents by fire or otherwise to goods while in bonded warehouse or on the quay and before delivery out of the charge of the Customs Department, the usual practice is not to charge duty on such portion of the goods as is proved to have been irretrievably lost or destroyed.

Tobacco on which duty has been paid. Except in cases of errors of account, no official cognizance is taken of such goods after they have been delivered out of the charge of the Customs Department and, consequently, no refund of duty from the Government can be counted upon in the event of the goods being destroyed by fire.

In these circumstances, an insurance should be effected for the full value of the goods including duty, and it will readily be understood that in the event of a fire occurring in or near any portion of the factory where a considerable quantity of stock is deposited (the leaf room, for example), the loss through fire, smoke, and water might be a serious one.

INDEX

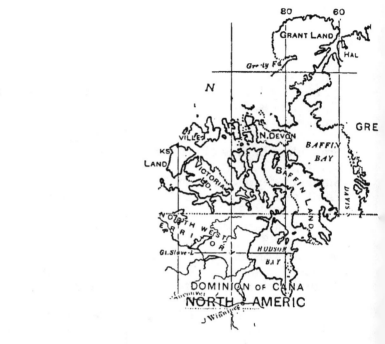

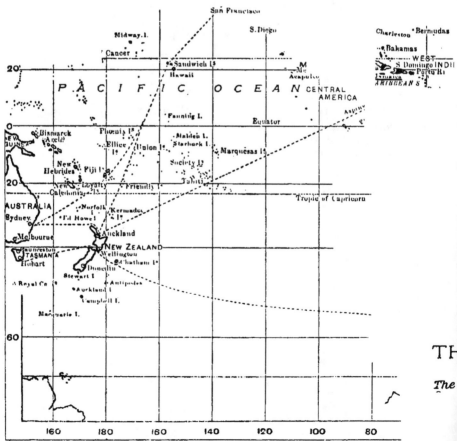

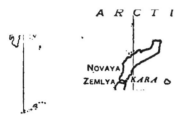

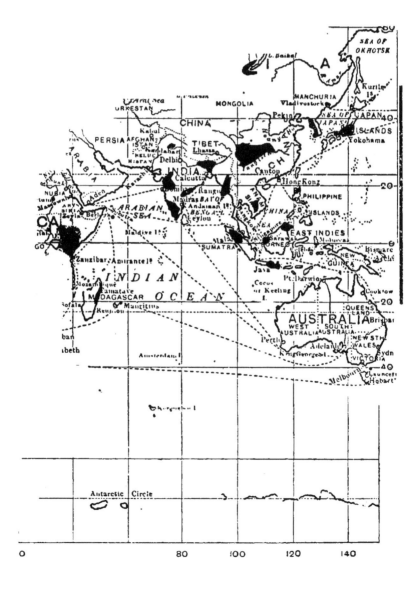

THE
RAW MATERIALS
OF COMMERCE

Edited by J. HENRY VANSTONE, F.R.G.S.

THIS up-to-date work, complete in two volumes, is intended for practical use in offices dealing with either the raw or manufactured products of the world. It is a detailed guide to the sources, classification, and other facts of the materials used in manufacture. The contents are carefully grouped to facilitate reference to the origin, nature, development, and use of all known products.

ABRIDGED CONTENTS

Vegetable Products

Fibres — Rubber — Oils — Fats — Drugs — Foods — Beverages — Gums — Resins — Dyes — Woods — Tobacco.

Animal Products

Fibres — Hides — Skins — Furs — Horns — Ivory — Pearls — Oils — Fats — Perfumes.

Mineral Products

Coal — Petroleum — Stone — Lime — Sands — Gravel — Clays — Precious Stones — Ores — Radium.

Synthetic Products

Coal Tar Derivatives — Celluloid — Synthetic Dyestuffs — Drugs — Chemicals — Casein — Resins.

"Well illustrated and produced, and should be welcomed in many quarters."—*London Chamber of Commerce Journal.*

"Should be on the desk or shelf of every business man and student of commerce."—*Nottingham Journal.*

"The author has succeeded in combining accuracy with the avoidance of unduly technical language."—*Nature.*

In two volumes, Size 11" × 8¾", Cloth gilt, 807 pp. Profusely illustrated.

20/-

NET
COMPLETE

Please send for a descriptive brochure, post free, on request.

SIR ISAAC PITMAN & SONS, LTD. PARKER STREET, KINGSWAY, W.C.2

CPSIA information can be obtained
at www.ICGtesting.com
Printed in the USA
BVHW041044040119
537043BV00014B/320/P

9 781332 241224